HUMANITY AT WORK

HUMANITY AT WORK

DIVERSITY, INCLUSION AND WELLBEING IN AN INCREASINGLY DISTRIBUTED WORKFORCE

ANJALI BINDRA PATEL, J.D.

NEW DEGREE PRESS

HUMANITY AT WORK

Diversity, Inclusion and Wellbeing in an Increasingly Distributed Workforce

ISBN   978-1-63676-507-5   *Paperback*

978-1-63676-027-8   *Kindle Ebook*

978-1-63676-028-5   *Ebook*

I dedicate this book to everyone whose phone still autocorrects their name.

CONTENTS

————

INTRODUCTION

———

You can't bury a memory and claim you've healed.

As I loaded my Subaru Loyale on that hot summer day in 1996, I felt a pang of anxiety. Starting law school might not be as risky as, say, camping on a cliff's edge, but I was still nervous about starting a new chapter in a new city.

As I drove toward the law school, I cranked up the mix CD that my best friend made for me and did something I rarely did- I exhaled. I had busted my butt to get to this point, and for the duration of that drive, I let myself appreciate the journey that had brought me here. I pushed aside the anxiety of being a shy girl in a completely new law school environment, assuring myself that everything would fall into place once I settled in.

In many ways, 1996 was a simpler time. Our interactions with one another were usually direct and in person. The internet was around, but I wasn't that familiar with it. No one I knew even owned a cellphone in those days. First impressions happened in person. To that end, I had spent the entire prior evening planning my "first day of school" outfit: a black blazer with jeans and an LL Bean backpack, hoping that I would somehow convey a mix of a seasoned professional and expert camper, though I was neither of those things.

Unlike my mom, I have always been someone who runs late and barely makes appointments on time, so I was surprised to find ample parking so close to the law school when I arrived for the first day of orientation. Was I at the wrong address? Where was everyone?

As I straightened the shoulder pads of my blazer and walked through the lobby of the law school, I realized that this particular orientation wasn't for the entire incoming class, but only for minorities. Almost everyone in the building that day was Black, Latinx, or Asian. We had a jump on everyone else and would spend the next few days walking through classrooms, meeting professors, and learning about the curriculum.

Similar to the feeling you get when someone calls you "Ma'am" before you feel you've reached the age to earn it, I couldn't decide if I was grateful or resentful for this special treatment. Yes, I enjoyed walking the halls of a school before classes started, but was this necessary? Would this early orientation give people the impression that I hadn't earned my place at the school?

It turns out that this wasn't just an internal debate I was having in my mind. When I walked back to my car mid-day, someone had plastered a note on the windshield of my

Subaru with a pathetic attempt at poetry: "Your Only Ahead Bc Your a Dot Head."

My eyes darted from left to right, scanning the parking lot. I wanted to confront the faceless attacker, but there was no one nearby. "It's 'you're,' not 'your,' you idiot!" I screamed tearfully in case the person was still lurking around. This was a pointless declaration because the only sounds around me were of my own rushed breathing and an abandoned McDonald's cup, skittering across the parking lot as the wind blew the cup from one empty parking spot to another. The sky was darkening, and I could smell the dampness in the air. A torrential downpour was moments away. I let the wind carry the note away, thinking that releasing the words from my hands would somehow also remove it from my memory.

I was hoping the note was a one-time thing, but it wasn't. At the end of the day, my stomach dropped as I approached my car and saw a crumpled piece of paper jammed into the driver's side door. My hands were shaking. Part of me was saying, *Don't open it—just throw it away,* but I couldn't resist. I opened it. A Subway receipt that had "GO HOME" scrawled on the back glared at me. I got in my car and just sat there, weighing my options. Should I report it? To whom? Did I really want to start school as "that brown girl who complains"? I told myself that this was just part of life and ended up suffering silently through the week, but the knowledge that someone was following me, and hated me without even knowing me, made me sick.

It's easy to tell someone to forget about a bad experience, but a lot harder to do it. When law school officially started,

I instinctively became uncomfortable whenever someone looked at me. *Was that the guy who plastered those hateful notes on my car?* I wondered when someone glanced at me as he walked by. *Is she sincere?* I would wonder when a woman smiled at me, "or is she the one who wanted me gone?"

The first few law school weeks were really challenging as I switched between feelings of anger and paranoia. My peace of mind had been shattered.

Orientation had set me apart, not for my hard work in college but for my skin color. I felt like an "other" and started treating perfectly well-intentioned people with a sense of suspicion, wondering if they had been the ones to track my car earlier in the year. My guard went up. Talking about the situation seemed totally out of the question, so I covered up my emotions. I wouldn't let anyone in. My sleep suffered. I felt completely off balance. My relationships, both in and out of school, suffered too.

As a naturally shy and introverted person, I was always that girl with her head stuck in a book. Openly discussing my feelings wasn't something that came naturally to me. Talking felt like reopening an old wound. I felt like I was all alone, that any complaints would make me seem weak or somehow partially to blame.

Times have changed since my law school days. My law school, and many others, now have an impressive myriad of diversity initiatives, from roundtables to diversity enrichment scholarships. Similarly, many organizations are now treating both diversity and inclusion as business imperatives rather than fringe benefits. After the systemic racism that killed George Floyd, Ahmaud Arbery, Breonna Taylor, Rayshard Brooks, and many others, racism and equality are finally front and center both in academic communities and in our national workplaces.

We all have an opportunity to learn more than we ever have and act more than we ever could: workplace culture shifts when we change our individual beliefs, our organizational customs, and our collective beliefs.

There is no better time to have uncomfortable conversations about how racism impacts our lives and how we can embrace diversity, inclusion, and belonging to improve our overall wellbeing both in and out of work. Have we been complicit in creating situations that we say we don't want? How can we change? Many leaders across various industries are already setting the standard for driving fundamental changes within their organizations and have successfully prioritized humanity. We need to understand what criteria they used and the plans they devised and implemented to achieve success; which organizational cultures embrace its people's life experiences and perspectives? And how can we adapt the same?

I felt I needed to write this book because when I look back on my experiences during law school and subsequent periods, I realized that more voices need to be heard. More experiences with diversity, inclusion, and wellbeing need to be shared. Diversity, inclusion, connection, and compassion are critical if we are going to improve our individual and collective landscapes, whether at a law school in the Midwest, a Fortune 500 company, or a start-up in Silicon Valley.

Humanity at Work is written from my perspective, as a Brown woman in an often Black and White world.

I was born in Cleveland, where my classmates described my skin tone as somewhere between a potato and peanut butter. That meant I would never be white enough to blend in at a Kid Rock concert (which I now regret attending for other reasons), but I'd never been brown enough to be considered a "complete" Indian.

As an Indian American woman, I have often been marginalized. I have also been blessed with privilege.

On the one hand, I've never had to teach my son that he shouldn't run across people's front yards because someone might find him suspicious and call the police. I've never had to familiarize myself with bicycle bell laws because my kids aren't Black and likely won't be stopped by the police for riding a bike without a bell in states like NJ, SC, NY, IN, and GA.

On the other hand, I've had people question my attendance at a 4th of July parade because this was "not my country" and "not my day." I've had my patriotism questioned in the presence of my two toddlers, even as my husband was deployed to Afghanistan, fighting on behalf of the very country I was accused of hating.

As a society and within our workplaces, we need to listen, learn, change, and understand that atrocities cannot be compartmentalized. Certain incidents, and the emotions and advocacy that follow, can't be left at home. They become ingrained in who we are.

Throughout this book, I speak as someone who is at once Indian, American, a mother, a daughter, a wife, a Gen X'er, a cisgender woman, a lawyer, and an advocate. I am part of, but don't speak on behalf of any of those identities. My personal stories and opinions come from my perspective, resulting from both my consistent oppression and fortunate privileges.

This book explores the intersections of diversity, inclusion, and wellbeing, both in the traditional office setting and remote and distributed workforces. Humanity at Work is directly relevant to people who want to optimize these convergences at work. It's for organizational leaders who want to learn how their team can be comfortable enough to bring their authentic selves to work and for those who want to create a space where differences can be accepted, embraced, and celebrated.

You will love this book if you are a manager dedicated to creating a better work environment for your team, a leader who wants to connect with her underrepresented team members or run a more united company, or someone who is generally passionate about diversity, inclusion, and wellbeing. This book will cite a lot of research, point to harsh realities, and recount hopeful stories from experts. This book is for you to gain awareness and tools to become a better advocate for humanity at work.

This book is also for people who experienced how work shifted from a *place* people go to a *thing* people do. Though the terms "remote" and "distributed" are used somewhat interchangeably in this book, the two terms are distinct. Remote work is a shift for an individual worker. It's an accommodation made for smaller groups of people, understanding that the majority are connected to an onsite location. Distributed workforces, which have increased in number in the age of COVID-19, refer to an entire workforce with no central location. In a distributed workforce, the focus is not on showing up physically, but rather on showing up mentally and socially from wherever you are located. Distributed workforces have undergone a total overhaul of collaboration and communication tools, work paradigms, social contracts, and training. This book is for anyone seeking a deeper understanding of why distributed work is inclusion work in today's environment and how teams, organizations, and entire communities can come together through distributed workforces.

Most importantly, this book is for anyone willing to get uncomfortable, have tough conversations, push for change, and optimize the true humanity in themselves and in those around them.

Part One gets into the "whats" of diversity, inclusion, and wellbeing. What is diversity, and how does it look in a traditional versus distributed setting? What are the various elements of our identities that we often feel are liabilities and need to be masked? What is inclusion, and how can we define wellbeing? What are the intersections of these concepts? What is the impact of the fact that millennials represent more than 50 percent of the total workplace?[1] Rapidly changing demographics indicate that America that will be

---

1   William H. Frey, "Diversity Defines the Millennial Generation," Brookings, June 28, 2016.

majority-minority by 2045. [2] What will be the risks and consequences of not attending to the issues of diversity, inclusion, and wellbeing, particularly when remote work allows our best talent to switch employers without ever leaving the comfort of their home offices? What is racism, and how does it impact our sense of inclusion, mental health, and overall wellbeing?

Part Two digs into the "whys" of diversity, inclusion, and wellbeing. Why do these concepts matter, and why should leaders work toward cultivating a stronger sense of belonging where people can bring their whole selves to work? Why are so many employees uncomfortable bringing their entire selves to work, and what is the cost of having them slowly disengage because of it? Why do both the business values and the moral values of an inclusive workplace matter? Why do these issues become even more relevant in a remote or distributed workplace? Why does exclusion, the opposite of inclusion, threaten to silence both majority and minority groups' voices? Why are some companies failing, while others are thriving, at building inclusive workplace cultures?

Part Three gets into the "hows" of diversity, inclusion, and wellbeing. This is the part of the book that offers substantive takeaways for both leaders and individuals. How can we change our behaviors and our actions to form a more inclusive and welcoming workplace? How can we inclusively recruit in both traditional and remote workplaces so we can graduate from a compliant workplace to an employer of choice? How can we avoid delegating the responsibilities of

---

2   William H. Frey, "The US will become 'minority white' in 2045, Census projects," Brookings, March 14, 2018.

inclusion solely to a designated diversity director, and how can each of us show true compassion and empathy for others' experiences? How can all of us identify our advantages and disadvantages, our privileges and our oppressions? How can we frame conversations so we are all included? How do we move from talking to doing?

Truth be told, I struggled with ordering the chapters of this book and almost put the "how" section first. Why? Because in today's world, we are at a point where we need to jump in and change our behaviors immediately. The whys and the whats are important, but when you see someone about to walk into oncoming traffic, your first instinct isn't to explain the ins and outs of crosswalks or the importance of looking both ways before you cross the street. Your first instinct is to yell, "STOP!"

In a similar vein, America is at a tipping point. We can't afford business as usual because we will lose our best talent, our important clients, and our own credibility if we don't do better. Leaders who don't embrace diversity and inclusion publicly and privately risk falling behind and alienating their best talent. Our immediate job as diversity and inclusion advocates is to prevent yet another professional and humanitarian calamity. We've seen too many missteps. We can't afford to wait any longer. We need to take corrective action right now, and Part Three will tell you exactly how to begin. In my time learning and teaching about diversity, inclusion, and wellbeing, something has become clear: understanding how to move through the journey of connecting people is the most important step for our evolution toward real and sustainable change.

PART ONE

THE "WHATS" OF DIVERSITY, INCLUSION, AND WELLBEING

CHAPTER ONE

WHAT IS DIVERSITY?

―――――

"Diversity: the art of thinking independently together."
― MALCOLM FORBES[3]

It's 2003. Imagine you're a guy named Hasan Minhaj, a senior in high school in Davis, California. You're not the most popular guy, and you're not the best ballplayer, but you have insane email skills, and you're good at math. The highlight of this new school year? Two words. Bethany Reed. She just moved from Nebraska and is in your AP Calculus class.[4]

You start messaging each other online. You become friends. You start studying at her house. Her parents like you: they always ask you how you're doing, they offer you brownies, and they regularly invite you to stay for dinner.

One day, Bethany shows up at *your* house to study. You're frazzled because your Indian background means that your

―――――

3   "Malcolm Forbes Quotes." Brainy Quote. Accessed September 5, 2020.
4   *Hasan Minhaj: Homecoming King,* directed by Christopher Storer (2017; Davis, CA; Netflix).

home life doesn't fit a typical American household's mold. There are no brownies in the oven- there are fresh *samosas* in the fryer. No one is watching *Friends* on tv —your parents are watching a Bollywood movie on ZeeTv. The daily chitchat? It's in Hindi.

After a few minutes of studying in your fully Indian house, Bethany looks up from her book. She says, "You know what? This is really nice. We should do this more often!" The anxiety you had been holding onto all evening starts melting.

As the spring quarter rolls around at school, Mr. Pendleton, your calculus teacher, dares the entire class to go to prom. "There's more to life than math. Live a little!" he advises.

The bell rings, and you hear the pitter-patter of Bethany's footsteps. "Listen," she says. "You've made my school year so memorable—will you go to prom with me?"

You know that prom is not a word used in your household. Unsure of how to broach the topic, you get home and just hit it directly. "Dad, I want to go to prom," you announce.

"Oh really, Hasan?" your dad says, "You want to go to prom? *Main tumhaara munh tod doonga!*" he screams. (This roughly translates to "I'm going to break your mouth.") Mentioning the word "prom" can be enough to set off a firestorm in an Indian household, but openly declaring your intention to go? Not a common or advisable approach.

Despite the parental shut down, you decide you'll do whatever it takes to make it to prom. The night of the dance, you put on your JC Penney suit, sneak out your bedroom window, and bike to Bethany's house, corsage in hand.

You've been to her house a million times, but this time is different. You take things in. You are about to go to prom with *Bethany Reed*. You ring the bell. Her mom answers. She opens the door, but she has a look of concern on her face. You look over her shoulder to see another guy putting a corsage on Bethany's wrist.

What is happening?

"Oh my gosh, honey," Bethany's mom said. "Did Bethany not tell you? Aw, sweetie, we love you. We love that you come over and study. But tonight's one of those nights where… well, we have a lot of family back at home in Nebraska… and we're gonna be taking a lot of photos tonight… so we don't think you will be a good fit…I'm so sorry…"

This was how political commentator and TV Host Hasan Minhaj shared his experience with senior prom in his 2017 Netflix special called *Homecoming King*. Still, what he felt that night is not unique: every single one of us, at some point, has been celebrated for adding a new dimension to an existing environment or has been shunned because of it.[5]

So, what is diversity? Ask different people, and you'll hear different responses, but one way to look at diversity is having or being composed of different elements. In other words, diversity is a range of different things. It's variety.

---

5   Ibid.

I wince when people look at me and call me a "diverse" person. A *person* isn't diverse. A team can be diverse. A community can be diverse. An organization can be diverse. My brown skin, taken alone as one individual, is not diverse. Diverse from what? From whom?

"Diversity is a relational concept," says Global Strategist Sarah Saska. "It shows up in the composition of teams and organizations and is measured based on a collective whole. In this way, diversity refers to differences within a given setting. While a person is not diverse, they may bring a diverse range of experiences, from appearance to thought, likes or dislikes, and identity. Diversity of identity may relate to socialized and visible race, gender identity, religion, nationality, body shape or size, age, or sexual orientation, to name a few."[6]

Consider what diversity means to you. You're right if you think about things like gender or race. Other types of traits that make for a diverse team include age, sexual orientation, and physical abilities. These are examples of inherent diversities.

There are other types of diversity as well, the ones acquired by experience: cross-cultural experiences, political beliefs, parental status, military backgrounds, and education are just a few. Diversity is a workforce of individuals with varying genders, religions, races, ages, ethnicities, physical abilities, sexual orientation, education, and other attributes in a work context. It's about the differences between people within your teams, company, and ecosystem.

---

6   Sarah Saska, "How to Define Diversity, Equity, and Inclusion at Work," Culture Amp, 2019.

What does diversity look and feel like? Diversity is variety. Diversity is discomfort. Diversity is tolerance. Diversity is opportunity.

Diversity matters, especially in our workforces, because it broadens our perspective, and it exposes us to views that are less explored in a homogenous society.

Going back to Hasan's story, let's assume for a minute that things had gone differently and that, despite Bethany's parents' reluctance, they allowed Hasan and Bethany to go to prom together. Would that have been any better in the long run?

When Hasan talks about his prom story on stage, he reflects: "I'd eaten off their plates. I'd kissed their daughter. I didn't know that people could be bigoted even as they were smiling at you."

Hasan's story depicts the effect of a lack of diversity. Whether it's based on cultural, racial, gender, education, or other characteristics, diversity is important because it helps eliminate negative stereotypes and personal biases about different groups of people. It helps us recognize and appreciate the many ways of being that are different from our own.

There's a saying that diversity is being asked to the party, and inclusion is being asked to dance. Diversity, then, is being let inside.

In Hasan's case, he never made it past the front door.

BREAKING DOWN DIVERSITY: THE PIECES VERSUS THE PUZZLE

You can use two somewhat opposing perspectives from which to view diversity. One approach emphasizes specific identifiers like ethnicity, race, gender, disability, and sexual orientation. If a person is a puzzle, the identifiers are the pieces.

The second approach is more of an intersectionality approach, which takes the identifiers into account, but sees people through a wider lens. If a person is a puzzle, then intersectionality looks at the completed puzzle. This intersectionality bleeds heavily into the concept of inclusion, and we'll dive deeper into this idea in the next chapter.

For now, let's look at some of the traditional diversity identifiers, which include but aren't limited to things like ethnicity, race, gender, disability, and sexual orientation. Why is it important to get familiar with these identifiers? Because there is still a long way to go to in corporate America:

- In 2013, less than 15 percent of the Fortune 500 executive officer positions were held by women.[7]
- In 2014, Fortune 500 CEOs were 95 percent white, 4.8 percent female, 2 percent Hispanic, 1.2 percent black, and 1.8 percent Asian.[8]

---

7   Rachel Soares and Liz Mulligan-Ferry, "Report: 2013 Catalyst Census: Fortune 500 Women Board Directors," Catalyst, December 10, 2013.

8   Chris Parker et al., "Where's the Diversity in Fortune 500 CEOs?" DiversityInc. October 8, 2012.

- There is one openly gay CEO among the Fortune 500 companies.[9]

Much has been done to further diversity in workplaces, but so much more needs to be done. The identifiers below, though not exhaustive, are some of the common markers employers have traditionally looked at:

DIVERSITY BASED ON ETHNICITY

September 11, 2001 is simple history for younger people, but for those who witnessed it, it's a dark memory that destroyed many optimistic views of the world. It's a day that's impossible to forget.

I was a young associate at a downtown Chicago law firm, and as usual, was rushing to get to work that Tuesday morning. The prior day had been excruciatingly long, and I was still a bit bleary-eyed when I walked into the office that morning. At first, I didn't notice the eerie silence permeating the air, but I could see the confusion and anxiety in people's eyes when I looked up. I followed their gaze to the TV nearby and watched nervously as journalist Bryant Gumbel came on the air, reporting a plane crash at the World Trade Center. At first, it seemed unclear what was happening, but a few short minutes into the coverage, our confusion turned to horror as a second plane crashed, this time into the South Tower building. "Oh no, oh no, oh no," another reporter was crying from a second TV in the office, "Another one just hit. This is

---

9   Emily Cohn, "Here Are All the Openly Gay CEOs In The Fortune 500," HuffPost, October 30, 2014.

a terror attack!" Not knowing what to do, many of us fled, leaving our things behind. We were in the hub of downtown Chicago and were terrified that we would be targeted next.

People were flooding the streets. I lived several miles away in Lincoln Park, and couldn't make it back to my apartment. I had no plan and wasn't sure where to go. I just knew I needed to get away from the large office buildings near me. I instinctively started running toward my friend Rajeev's apartment, which was nearby. We sat together all day, alternating between watching live coverage, crying, and worrying about our friends and family. Rajeev's brother worked in NYC, but no one had heard from him all day. By evening, Rajeev had finally tracked down his little brother. He was okay.

In the coming days, a stunning silence gripped the nation as people wondered, "What comes next?" As news coverage increased and more faces flashed across the screen, the phrase "It's a new kind of war with a new kind of enemy," began circulating. I had the terrifying realization that many of those terrorists, these new kinds of enemies, looked a little bit like our own community members. This scared me because I knew I wasn't the only one who noticed the resemblances.

I can't pinpoint exactly when the "othering" started for me, but potential clients increasingly started asking me: "What languages do you speak? What is your religion? Does your religion allow you to drink? What holidays do you celebrate?" My professional advancement suddenly seemed to be hinging on my responses. I'd be lying if I didn't admit that I attempted to pass myself off as Hispanic on a few occasions. Anyone from Southeast Asia or the Middle East region seemed to fall into the nebulous "Arab" descriptor in the days following 9/11. While at work, I tried my hardest to mask any identifiers that linked me back to that.

That was my first serious lesson that my differences in a community of local lawyers were being noticed. This was my first lesson in culture and how it felt to be rejected by it. I just couldn't see myself being able to progress professionally while maintaining my personal identity. I spent almost as much time covering up or masking parts of myself as I did working. I grew tired. I slowly disengaged. Two years later, I left Chicago.

I thought back to the days when my parents first came to the USA in the late 1960s. My dad, an organic chemist, recalled the frequent interactions where acquaintances would casually ask him, "So, when do you plan to go back?"

Thirty-something years later, that's kind of how I felt too.

My race may have made me a minority, but my decision to leave my job was far from unique. Up to 70 percent of people, regardless of their race, are disengaged at work. If you think your company/firm is safe, pause, and think again. Seven of the ten people on the elevator with you are disengaged and actively looking for new jobs, and one of them might soon be you.[10]

---

10   Marcel Schwantes, "A New Study Reveals 70 Percent of Workers Say They are Actively Looking for a New Job. Here's the Reason in 5 Words," Inc, December 4, 2018.

It's been nearly twenty years since my young lawyer experience, but even today, companies and professions aren't as diverse as they need to be. Intuitively, we know that diversity matters and that different perspectives lead to innovation and connection. Despite the benefits of diversity, there's still a perception gap about how important it actually is.

Accenture's recent report, based on a global survey of more than 30,000 professionals in 28 countries, found that diversity just isn't a top strategic priority for the majority of leaders.[11] Many companies will continue to hire through their networks, which often reflect the same race, gender, and ethnicity in top leadership positions.

Diversity statements may get recognition via social media posts, but the money to support these initiatives may be overtaken by financial performance and brand recognition (76 percent and 72 percent, respectively) as top strategic priorities; meanwhile, 34 percent of leaders ranked diversity a top priority.[12] There will be a price to pay for ignoring diversity, which we will cover in more detail in this book's "whys" section.

DIVERSITY BASED ON RACE

To solve a problem, you first have to recognize that it exists.

Achieving racial equity in the workplace will be an essential issue for organizations to tackle in the days and years ahead.

---

11   Sheryl Estrada, "Diversity, culture not a top strategic priority for most leaders," HR Dive, March 4, 2020.

12   *Ibid.*

Too often, our conditioning leads us to believe that minority hiring is a concession, not an asset. To break down and eliminate this dangerous misconception, we need to talk about racism before we get into diversity. We can't embrace one without understanding the other.

It's impossible to talk deeply about diversity without also addressing racism and discrimination. We can overcome a lack of diversity by throwing bodies into an office. We can even ask people to treat each other respectfully. But increased representation, if void of strategy to combat racism and discrimination, won't solve anything. Until organizations and people realize that diversity benefits the organization more than any one individual, it will be difficult to sustain real momentum.

Merriam Webster defines racism as a belief that race is the primary determinant of human traits and capacities and that racial differences produce an inherent superiority of a particular race.[13]

Race talks make us uneasy, but this conflict has to be part of the conversation with racism and diversity. I've seen many companies try to approach issues from a "race neutral" perspective, but that hardly seems effective. Our race is a large part of who we are and pretending that it isn't is both ineffective and insincere.

No one person is a race representative for an entire group of people. As an Indian American, it's not my responsibility,

---

13   *Merriam-Webster*, s.v. "Race (n.)," accessed July 27, 2020.

or even my right, to speak on behalf of all Indian people. Nor is it anyone's job to share every personal story, run every diversity initiative, or teach every employee about the importance of anti-racism and diversity, particularly when it's expected to happen without additional recognition and pay.

Diversity and humanity in the workplace come from giving people the ability to work with their entire backgrounds and experiences being acknowledged.

In the wake of George Floyd's murder, many companies posted about the importance of diversity- my newsfeed was flooded with well-intentioned comments. Companies went public with their intentions to embrace diversity. The problem? Some companies claim the benefit of action, a commitment to diversity, without actually following through. In other words, a blackout square on Instagram or a signature on a diversity pledge can prematurely let people off the hook. Diversity is not mere intention—diversity is action.[14]

DIVERSITY BASED ON DISABILITY

RespectAbility, an organization that fights stigma against disabilities, reports that one in five people have a disability in the US today.[15] What does diversity for the disabled community look like, and how do we move past the uncomfortable conversations into affirmative progress?

---

14 David Bindon et al.,"Policy Proposal: An Anti-Racist West Point," Slideshare, June 25, 2020.

15 Jennifer Calfas. "CDC: 1 in 5 American Adults Live with a Disability." Mississippi Department of Rehabilitation Services. July 31, 2015.

First, companies need to have deeper conversations about different types of disabilities and discrimination that often plagues each type.

On the topic of disabilities, I was pleasantly surprised to see inspiration come from the most unexpected places: television. When the quarantine of 2020 was just beginning, our family, like many others, took comfort in a reliable companion: Netflix. My kids stumbled on a show called *The Healing Powers of Dude*, a comedy about a middle schooler with a social anxiety disorder.[16]

Respectability.org points to the National Alliance on Mental Illness (NAMI), which lists anxiety as the most common health disorder in the US. Although general anxiety is classified as normal, anxiety disorders are more difficult to cope with. Eighteen percent of adults and eight percent of children in the US have an anxiety disorder.[17] "The more families and friends can talk about this issue, the better the chance people can get the help they need," *Healing Powers* creators Erica Spates and Sam Littenberg-Weisberg told RespectAbility.[18]

RespectAbility teamed up with the show's creators to develop another character, Amara, Noah's fearless friend who uses a wheelchair. "There are disabilities you can see, like someone in a wheelchair, and those you might never know about,

---

16 *The Healing Power of Dude,* created by Sam Littenberg-Weisberg, and Erica Spates, January 13, 2020.

17 "Mental Illness, including Anxiety, Bipolar Disorder, Depression and More," Respectability, accessed July 30, 2020.

18 Lauren Appelbaum, "Netflix's Newest Series Takes Disability Inclusion to a New Level," Respectability, January 13, 2020.

like anxiety. We decided this could be a great opportunity to show kids and families the struggles people face on both sides and challenge some of the prejudices and misconceptions people have... representation is very important to us, as well as to Netflix," said Spates and Littenberg-Weisberg, "We understand the power of seeing yourself represented in media and that the more you see it, the more it can become commonplace."[19]

Healing Powers of Dude should be required viewing for everyone in the adult workforce. The media often overlook disabilities, and people with disabilities often don't get the attention or opportunities they deserve. Diversity means including those with disabilities, focusing on securing their rights, supporting their needs, and implementing accommodations.

DIVERSITY BASED ON AGE

Age diversity is the acceptance of all age groups in the workforce.

Forbes reports that although workers over 40 are a protected class under the Age Discrimination in Employment Act, two-thirds of people between the ages of 45 and 74 report discrimination based on age. One-fifth of discrimination charges filed with the federal Equal Employment Opportunity Commission is based on age.[20]

---

19 Lauren Appelbaum, "Cast of Hollywood Changemakers Fight Stigmas During Americans with Disabilities Act Celebration," July 24, 2020.

20 Kimberly Palmer, "10 Things You Should Know About Age Discrimination," AARP, February 20, 2017.

Many companies see older workers as a competitive disadvantage, which left me speechless.[21] I still rely on my father for sage advice on issues ranging from taxes to parenting. He is nearly 80 and one of the sharpest people I know. On a broader note, every US president has been over the "old" age of 40 at the start of their terms, so it's puzzling that we trust an older worker to run the nation but somehow see them as a disadvantage at work.

On the other side of the spectrum, over a third of today's workforce—more than 56 million people—are of the millennial and post-millennial generation or Generation Z.[22] By 2025, this group will make up nearly 75 percent of the workforce.[23] Once we wrap our heads around these staggering numbers, it only makes sense to examine the impact this largest (and growing) segment will have on the future workplace, especially in the realm of diversity and inclusion.[24]

Employers who want to compete for the best Gen Z talent should prioritize diverse workplace cultures from a hiring perspective. A Feb. 18, 2020 report from Alexander Mann found that Gen Z employees think diversity should include age, ethnicity, disability, gender, religion, sexual orientation, and elements such as socioeconomic background,

21 Josh Bersin and Tomas Chamorro-Premuzic, "The Case for Hiring Older Workers," Harvard Business Review, September 26, 2019.

22 Richard Fry, "Millennials are the largest generation in the US labor force," Pew Research Center, April 11, 2018.

23 "Big Demands and High Expectations: The Deloitte Millennial Survey," Deloitte, January 2014.

24 Nish Parikh, "Diversity And Inclusion Matters To The Workforce Of The Future," Forbes, May 9, 2018.

educational background, geographic location, work style, ideology, and lived experiences.[25]

While it's not fair to generalize that Gen Z cares more about diversity than past generations, it's clear that Gen Z is more likely to be exposed to diverse groups of people- so if companies want the best talent, they need to care too and do something about it.[26]

DIVERSITY BASED ON SEXUAL ORIENTATION

LGBTQIA (lesbian, gay, bisexual, transgender, queer, intersex, asexual) people are more visible in society than in the workforce, which needs to be addressed.

Employers worldwide have considered the economic benefits of becoming an LGBTQIA friendly workplace, and many of them voluntarily enacted a range of policies, including those prioritizing non-discrimination practices. To affirm diverse identities within the lesbian, gay, bisexual, transgender (LGBT) community, the workplace has to evolve with current perspectives on language that more accurately captures anyone who identifies as part of this community.

DIVERSITY BASED ON GENDER

Gender diversity is a fair and equitable representation of people from different genders. It usually refers to an equitable ratio of men and women but also includes nonbinary genders.

---

25   Valerie Bolden Barrett, 2020. *Gen Z Seeks Cognitive Diversity At Work.* [online] HR Dive, February 25, 2020.

26   "The Nielsen Total Audience Report: Q1 2017," Nielsen, July 12, 2017.

Gender diversity at work means that all genders are hired at consistent rates, are paid equally, and are given the same working, leadership, and promotional opportunities.

And there's the rub. According to data from the US Census Bureau, the average gender pay gap in the United States in 2018 was around 18.9 percent, meaning that a woman working a full-time, year-round job earns 81.1 percent as much as her male counterparts, with nonbinary genders not even taken into account.[27]

There's a lot to be said about the impact of these wage discrepancies, and we are going to get into all of it in future chapters.

DIVERSITY BASED ON EXPERIENCES AND BACKGROUND

Diversity based on experiences, like being in the military, can offer employers a wealth of skills, knowledge, and experience. Varying backgrounds in education and work experience also make for a diverse workforce. Each time an employee moves into a new job, industry, or company, they bring their own unique set of work experiences and skills with them. A consultant based in Cleveland will likely have an entirely different arsenal of communication tools than a consultant based in Shanghai. Similarly, variances in educational backgrounds can also be an asset. Case in point: one of my favorite college professors spent over 16 years working as a hairdresser. He

---

27 Occupation By Sex And Median Earnings In The Past 12 Months (in 2018 Inflation-Adjusted Dollars) For The Full-Time, Year-Round Civilian Employed Population 16 Years And Over," United States Census Bureau, 2018.

said he learned more about creative communication and time management at the salon than he ever learned while getting his teaching degree.

Individual differences, whether external or internal, help provide workplace environments where innovation and ideas can thrive.

DIVERSITY IN AN INCREASINGLY DISTRIBUTED WORKFORCE

As COVID-19 changes how we work in the 21st century, we have an unprecedented opportunity to embrace diversity, and all that remote and flexible workforces have to offer. Our response to the COVID-19 outbreak has seen a large increase in remote work. Distributed workforces may become the new normal, even after the pandemic ends. That's a silver lining to the pandemic, but also more gloomy news too: a 2020 survey shows that 27 percent of companies have put their diversity initiatives on hold as part of the pandemic response.[28]

Putting diversity initiatives on the back burner is a mistake. Remote work gives us an unprecedented opportunity to diversify our workforce:

- Looking at a hiring need from a remote perspective immediately requires a focus on skills and aptitudes, instead of our 'who do we know that...' approach, which

---

28   Kevin Dolan et al., "Diversity During COVID-19 Still Matters." McKinsey & Company. May 19, 2020.

lets us learn about a candidate from their application rather than on connections alone.

- Remote work allows people with physical and sensory disabilities to take over a wide range of roles and brings another layer of diversity to a company's culture.
- Allowing people to work remotely could be a lifesaving change for older workers or those with autoimmune disorders who may be more vulnerable to COVID-19.

Remote work allows us to embrace people *where they are* for *who they are* and gives them the opportunity to do their best work from the comfort of their homes and communities.

CONCLUSION

Accenture's report "Getting to Equal 2020: The Hidden Value of Culture Makers," a global survey of more than 30,000 professionals in 28 countries in 2020, found that diversity is not a top strategic priority for the majority of leaders because they seem to believe they already have a favorable company culture and things are already going well: their "check the box" mentality makes them think that yes, they are diverse, and things are going well, even when they aren't.[29]

This needs to change.

When it comes to diversity, progress will be determined by how quickly CEOs can pivot from saying to doing. American corporations have spent a long time talking about addressing

---

29 Julie Sweet et al., "Getting to Equal 2020: The Hidden Value of Culture Makers," Accenture, 2020.

the barriers underrepresented groups face in the workplace, but key indicators ranging from employment numbers to representation in management show that not enough has been done. A lot of long-term goals need to take on short-term urgency. As of 2020, more than 10 percent of companies use diversity as a formal metric in incentive schemes, but in the wake of George Floyd's murder, a lot more organizations will begin to consider prioritizing it.[30]

Diane Hoskins, Co-CEO of architectural firm Gensler, says that setting specific, measurable, and achievable goals doesn't necessarily require a lot of time. "I think you'd be surprised how fast we can come up with them." She said instead of a quota system, which is both legally and morally questionable, HR departments need to focus on attracting, developing and retaining the right people.[31]

Employers should consider diversity as one factor in their overall assessment of a candidate, not the sole criterion. Diversity is one of many individualized considerations about a candidate. The goal isn't to diversify by offering positions to less qualified candidates. The goal is to open the door wide enough so all qualified candidates (based on traditional résumé skills and life skills and perspectives) can find the space to walk inside.

30 John D. Stoll, "For CEOs, Pressure Is On to Pivot From 'Say' to 'Do' on Inequality." The Wall Street Journal. June 26, 2020.

31 Ibid.

CHAPTER TWO

WHAT IS INCLUSION?

———

"Should I walk in the room and leave the gay out of the room, or leave the black out of the room? For most of my career, I've had some variation of this question. I think the way to talk about being black and gay is to talk about being whole, being a whole being."[32]

– ROBERT O'HARA

When I was in fourth grade, I received my first invite to a classmate's birthday party. Kristy's party would be princess-themed, and we were all supposed to bring our favorite dolls. I was more of a stuffed animal girl, but I was lucky enough to have one doll, and she looked a lot like me. She had long black hair, a red sari, and a *bindi* on her forehead. Her name, as listed on the box, was simply: Indian Barbie.

When I arrived at the party, Kristy's mom was lining up a bunch of wrapped packages on top of their pinball machine.

---

32   Robert O'Hara, "Artist Interview with Robert O'Hara," interview by Tim Sanford, Playwrights Horizons, accessed November 10, 2014.

"Good news, girls!" Kristy's mom said. "Everyone here is going home with a prize- either small, medium, or large. What you win depends on how many votes you get!" Votes? Votes for what? As if she could hear my inner panic, Kristy's mom straightened her Jordache jeans and pointed to a makeshift stage, which consisted of some pallets covered with cardboard and tablecloths. Apparently, we were all supposed to go up there, one by one, and explain why our doll was the most beautiful princess at the party (It was 1984 in Cleveland, okay?)

My stomach dropped. I was painfully shy, and public speaking was barely preferable to diving headfirst into a hornet's nest. The first few girls went up and giggled as they showed various versions of their blond-haired, blue-eyed mermaids and Cinderellas.

When it was my turn, I took Indian Barbie up with me and explained what a sari was.

"Why is your doll wearing a towel?" one girl snickered.

"Her skin looks like dirt. She's so ugly!" my neighbor Adrienne laughed. At that point, I had no idea if she was directing that comment at Indian Barbie or me, but I was too mortified to wait to find out. I mumbled something inaudibly and ran off the stage.

The rest of the party was excruciating. Needless to say, I didn't win the princess contest. Kristy's mom gave me a "small" prize, a two-legged stuffed brown dog with his tongue sticking out. Truth be told, I thought the dog was awesome and should have been in the "large" prize category, but I took my wins where I could find them.

After Kristy's mom passed around the pepperoni pizza (which I couldn't eat because I'm vegetarian), she dimmed the kitchen lights and started a dance party. Every song on the playlist was by the boy band of the year, Wham. When "Careless Whisper" came on, and George Michael started cooing, all the girls grabbed a partner and pretended to slow dance with each other. I stood alone near the back, eating some stale Ritz crackers Kristy's mom graciously dug up when she realized I couldn't have the pizza. I took some solace in the fact that my mom would be picking me up soon since I wasn't allowed to sleep over. Kristy's mom sat with me as I peered anxiously through their mustard yellow living room curtains, waiting to be rescued.

After a few minutes, I could see the blinding headlights of my mom's forest green 1978 Ford LTD approaching. At night, her car reminded me of a snake that had eerily morphed into a first-generation Transformer, but I was relieved to see the green monstrosity anyway. I quickly said bye to Kristy's mom and left through their garage, which smelled like birthday candles and grass. I walked over to their trash can and forcefully hurled Indian Barbie into their garbage. Indian Barbie's plastered princess smile peeked out through a pile of half-eaten pizza crusts and Twinkie wrappers. Her almond eyes suddenly seemed desperate, pleading with me to spare her the fate of a lifetime in a dumpster. I stared back at her, and without an ounce of remorse, I took the pink napkin I had been balling up in my sweaty hands, tossed it over her face, and slammed the lid shut. I clutched my new two-legged dog, knowing that unlike Indian Barbie, he would never betray me.

That birthday party was a literal example of the analogy about being asked to the party but not being asked to dance. It's the perfect example of having the diversity, but not the inclusion. It doesn't matter if it's a 10-year-old's birthday party or a position at a large company. Being let inside is great—it's a measurable metric that we can all see and talk about. But what happens after that?

Taking this idea of being "asked to dance" into a workplace setting, it seems that inclusion efforts and initiatives have stalled, partly because inclusion can be hard to measure and even harder to implement. In the last chapter, we touched on various identifiers of diversity: race, gender, disability, age, ethnicity, and so many others. These are the identifiers that help companies say they have diversity within their organizations.

Inclusion, though, is about more than being let inside. It's about more than standing around the back of someone's proverbial kitchen. Inclusion is about communication and involvement where employees are engaged, empowered, and together.

Belonging is when an employee feels valued, both as an employee and as a person. At many of my consulting talks, I use a basketball analogy. Diversity would be letting me play on the Cleveland Cavaliers as a forty-something Indian woman. Inclusion would be passing me the ball. Belonging? That's asking me about my kids or wishing me a Happy

Diwali; it shows that you both hear and appreciate all aspects of me, Indian Barbie and all.

INCLUSION IS ACCEPTANCE AND LISTENING

My story about the 4th-grade party shows what inclusion doesn't include, but what about what inclusion *does* include? Inclusion in the workplace boils down to welcoming, respecting, supporting, and valuing any individual or group's authentic participation. The workforce is changing, and it's changing fast. What often gets lost in the conversation is inclusion and how to create and maintain it.

An inclusive workplace understands the needs of its employees. It makes employees feel valued and heard and positively influences a person's longevity with an employer. According to The Society for Human Resource Management, inclusion is "the achievement of a work environment in which all individuals are treated fairly and respectfully, have equal access to opportunities and resources, and can contribute fully to the organization's success."[33]

The first step toward inclusion includes listening to and accepting different viewpoints from a wide range of individuals, including those in a majority group. This is often easier said than done if social media is any indication of workplace behavior.

In June of 2020, I saw a powerful post by Laura Silva, a LinkedIn connection posting about the importance of having

---

33   "Diversity & Inclusion," SHRM-LI, accessed July 28, 2020.

companies do more than talk. She was imploring companies to provide proof of diversity, equity, and inclusion, asking employers to "show the receipts." Her post quickly went viral.[34]

I hit the "like" button and started reading comments.

Many comments were positive, but I was stunned by people attacking Laura's post. "You're racist!" one commenter remarked. "Fascist!" said another, bashing her insistence that companies prove they care instead of just saying they do.

Some people quickly jumped in to defend Laura's post, including one white man, JH, who talked about Martin Luther King, Jr., and the need to end racism.

His comment opened the door to a new attack, this time against JH and his white privilege. People told him that he had no right to be part of the conversation and couldn't possibly understand what the original author was writing about.[35]

I reached out to JH to express my dismay at his attackers. He shared some of his personal struggles. We both talked. We both listened. I posted a comment defending his right to speak as a white man. Within minutes, my direct message notifications started going off. One person said my words reminded her of someone who was "just like a terrorist", while another called me a sell-out for defending JH. Huh? Since when is including everyone who wants to be part of

---

34 Laura Silva, "To the companies, I am not applauding your #blacklivesmatter post," Linkedin, June 2020.

35 Ibid.

a conversation, regardless of their backgrounds, a symbol of terrorism?

The entire LinkedIn interaction reminded me of Nikki Haley, former South Carolina governor and US Ambassador to the UN. She said:

"People talk about diversity more than ever, but too many of us are becoming intolerant in the name of tolerance. Instead of trying to understand those who disagree with us, we tend to write them off as not even fit to have a conversation with."[36]

"Inclusion matters" is a great message. But all of us, regardless of skin color, race, or background, need to be part of the solution. To Haley's point, haven't we all earned the right and the responsibility to do what's right, together?

Too many people opt out of vital conversations about diversity and inclusivity because they are worried about looking, speaking, or seeming wrong. The problem with shutting down opposing viewpoints is that it shatters our ability to work through issues and connect. Inclusion is not a zero-sum game. It doesn't have to be one or another. In fact, it can't be.

I recently worked with a law firm to launch a new women's initiative. Right out of the gate, the chief marketing officer made it a point to say that the firm wanted to handle the launch inclusively, so people would know that everyone's voice mattered—nothing about the launch centered around

---

36 Nikki R.Haley, *With All Due Respect: Defending America with Grit and Grace*, New York: St. Martin's Press, 2019.

an "us" versus "them" mindset. On the contrary, they wanted all genders present, all opinions heard, and all concerns addressed. The firm created a sense of psychological safety and belonging and sent the message that it's okay to speak up and work through differences.

That's how you embrace inclusion.

INCLUSION IS SPEAKING UP WHEN NEEDED AND PAYING ATTENTION WITHOUT BEING ASKED

Have you ever gone to a meeting where as soon as a woman starts speaking, the men in the room start looking down at their phones? How about stating an idea aloud, being ignored, and then hearing a male coworker regurgitate the same idea? Have you been spoken over or fallen victim to mansplaining, where a man condescendingly explains something that often isn't even accurate? If you've been there, you're not alone. In fact, even Supreme Court justices haven't been spared. Studies showed that female Supreme Court justices were interrupted three times as often as their male counterparts over a 12- year period.[37]

As we work toward building inclusive environments, we need to know when to stay silent, when to pay attention, and when to speak up.

The examples cited above are great times to be inclusive by being silent, but there are plenty of circumstances where

---

37   Tonja Jacobi et al., "Female Supreme Court Justices Are Interrupted More by Male Justices and Advocates," Harvard Business Review, April 11, 2017.

speaking up is the best way to support inclusion. Pay equity and microaggressions are good places to start.

PAY INEQUITIES

Everyone in the workforce has the right to expect equal pay for equal work regardless of their gender, race, religion, national origin, age, or physical/mental abilities. But not everyone is paid equally. The two types of wage gaps are the uncontrolled wage gap and the controlled wage gap.

The controlled wage gap controls every factor imaginable: education, industry, job title, city, etc. One would think that pay would be equal here, in this day and age, but it isn't. The controlled pay gap varies between 94 and 98 cents on the dollar, which means that someone named Kristy will make 94-98 cents while a man named Kris with the same credentials and years of service will get $1.00 for the same work.[38] Doesn't sound like a big deal? Multiply that wage gap by the number of hours you work per week and multiply that by 52. Now multiply that number by the number of years you plan to be in the workforce. If you still don't think it's a big deal, I have a bridge I'd like to sell you. I'll tell you the price once you tell me about your gender.

An uncontrolled wage gap compares all working women to all working men. The uncontrolled gender pay gap is 81 cents on the dollar, depending on the state.[39] The uncontrolled

38 "The State of the Gender Pay Gap in 2020." Payscale. Accessed September 5, 2020.

39 Robin Bleiweis, "Quick Facts About the Gender Wage Gap," American Progress, March 24, 2020.

gap doesn't control things like job level or experiences, so it can be confusing when people cite the 81 cents and follow it up with "unequal pay for equal work" without further explanation.

But it's equally misleading to leave that number at face value and jump right to controlled wages. Why? Because many biases come into play, from gender and racial bias in promotions to early bias against genders in certain careers.[40] Women often aren't part of the "in" group, never hear about the opportunities, and never get to capitalize on them.

When it comes to feeling a sense of inclusion, feeling valued is a huge part of the equation. How would any one of us feel if we knew that our gender, or our race, was the reason we were being paid less? Leadership needs to speak up and correct course before they lose their most valuable employees.

MICROAGGRESSIONS

Microaggressions are more than just callous or insensitive comments. Their venom comes from the fact that comments stem from another person's membership in an underrepresented or frequently harassed group. The comments are usually casual and small, and they happen frequently. Microaggressions are tiny little assaults, like a small drip from your faucet. Maybe it's not a big deal in isolation, but if you keep looking away, you may one day walk into your house to see that your entire kitchen has flooded.

---

40 Maria Danilova, "Study Shows Gender Bias at an Early Age," Boston Globe, January 26, 2017.

As microaggressions pile on top of each other, you start wondering what's so "micro" about it—it doesn't feel little when it happens every day—the weight of the anxiety, frustration, and fatigue can get unbearably heavy.

Here is a small sampling of microaggressions I've experienced, from oddly specific to infuriating:

- Micro-aggressor: "Hey, Anjali, can I ask you something? Why do all Indian parents recycle Dannon yogurt containers and cookie tins?"
- Micro-aggressor: "Hey Anjali, you must know this stuff. Can you help Alex with this Geometry problem?" (All Indians are not good at math. I got a C in Geometry and often struggle to help my middle-schooler with his math homework. How does that make me qualified?)
- Micro-aggressor: "Where are you from?" Me: "I'm from Cleveland." Micro-aggressor: "No, where are you FROM?" Me: "I came from my parents." Micro-aggressor: "Where are your parents from? I'm trying to figure out what you are."
- Micro-aggressor: "Anjali, you can take notes, right?" (When I'm the only female in the room).
- Micro-aggressor: "Can you translate this?" (Showing me a document written in Farsi. I'm not Persian.)
- Micro-aggressor: "Your husband has a job. Shouldn't you be home taking care of the kids?" (Heard this one from more than one Indian Auntie on more than one occasion.)

I am not always the victim of microaggressions; I've also been the inflictor. Looking back, I'm really embarrassed that I said these things, but maybe you can learn from my mistakes. Here are a few microaggressions I remember, though I'm sure I'm guilty of many more:

- Me: "Wow, you're good at this!" (Speaking in a surprised tone to a female contractor working on a construction project).
- Me: "You look gorgeous. You look like Lucy Liu!" My friend: "I'm not Chinese. I'm Korean."
- Overhearing two of my friends, one Black (Derrick) and one White (Dave), talking about getting coached for basketball. Me: "Derrick, can you coach my son too?" (Derrick wasn't coaching; Dave was).

Microaggressions may not be intentional or malicious, but that doesn't mean they aren't harmful. Constantly being subjected to microaggressions is like death by a thousand paper cuts. It's painful. Speaking up against microaggressions, or learning from your own, leads to trust and respect and produces a level of confidence in others that they won't be alienated or excluded for being themselves.

These conversations aren't always easy. They can get awkward and embarrassing, as they were when I was called out for my own inappropriate comments, but honest conversations about these issues aren't about being right or wrong. They're about exposing yourself to different perspectives and hearing what everyone has to say. They're about confronting reality, no matter what it looks like. Vulnerability is a part of that— it's saying," I'm here right now, and I'm hearing what you are saying." When we continue to have these talks, we will slowly become more comfortable bringing our full selves to work.

Inclusion means that it's okay to bring your whole self to work. We pay a lot of lip service to the idea, but how many companies really support the slogan? "Bringing our whole selves to work means showing up authentically, leading with humility, and remembering that we're all vulnerable, imperfect human beings doing the best we can. It's also about having the courage to take risks, speak up, ask for help, genuinely connect with others, and allowing ourself to be truly seen. It's not always easy for us to show up this way, especially at work. And it takes commitment, intention, and courage for leaders and organizations to create environments that are conducive to this type of authenticity and humanity," according to author Mike Robbins.[41] People desperately want to be part of something bigger and be connected, but they don't want to sacrifice their authenticity to do it.

Inclusion through speaking up and listening means that we won't feel we have to make ourselves smaller over time, and we won't feel like we need to modify who we are, how we look, or what we believe in order to make others more comfortable. It means that if you're the parent of three young kids and the school nurse calls because she is worried your child might be having an allergic reaction, you won't have to downplay your fear. You won't have to make up excuses about why you need to leave. It means you'll be able to openly say, "At this moment, my kids are the only things that matter, and I'll be back to work once I know they are okay."

---

41   Mike Robbins, *Bring Your Whole Self to Work: How Vulnerability Unlocks Creativity, Connection, and Performance*, Carlsbad: Hay House, 2018.

BELONGING IS WHAT MAKES INCLUSION STICK

Speaking up against microaggressions and listening when someone needs to be heard are critical parts of inclusion. But what is belonging? Is it the same thing as inclusion? No, but belonging is inextricably linked to inclusion. When people feel included and feel like they belong, they will be happier, more productive, and work to stay in their jobs longer. More than 80 percent of employees consider cultural fit a top priority.[42]

So, what is belonging? A team of behavioral scientists at BetterUp Labs defines belonging as "a close cousin to many related experiences: mattering, identification, and social connection. The unifying thread across these themes is that they all revolve around the sense of being accepted and included by those around you."[43] Think of inclusion as an action and belonging as a feeling.

Many of us spend more time at work than we do with our families, so we must be able to create a sense of belonging and community. It's important for us to feel like we matter. Belonging is when you feel safe and valued for embracing what makes you different.[44]

The bad news is that many organizations fail at the belonging piece. Forty percent of people say that they feel isolated

42 Lauren A. Rivera, "Guess Who Doesn't Fit In at Work," The New York Times, May 30, 2015.

43 Evan W. Carr et al., "The Value of Belonging at Work," Harvard Business Review, December 16, 2019.

44 John Baldoni, "Fostering The Sense of Belonging Promotes Success," Forbes, January 22, 2017.

at work.[45] The result? Embarrassingly lower commitment and engagement.[46] US businesses spend nearly 8 billion dollars each year on diversity and inclusion (D&I) training that miss the mark because they neglect our need to feel included.[47] What are we doing wrong?[48]

In June of 2020, the LA Times reported multiple instances of Black and Brown tech workers who had experienced discrimination on the job. In one instance, a Black career IT professional nominated himself for a promotion but was instead asked to help recruit another candidate, who was White. A Black Google engineer was physically confronted by a White coworker demanding to see his ID badge. A Black programmer on a contract was denied a full-time job and asked to train her unqualified White replacement instead."[49]

This lack of belonging and exclusion hurts, not just as emotional pain but as physical pain.[50]

We've all felt the burn of exclusion at some point. It's a horrible feeling, one that is gut-wrenchingly difficult, which means that belonging isn't just an issue for underrepresented groups:

---

45   Karyn Twaronite, "The Surprising Power of Simply Asking Coworkers How They're Doing," Harvard Business Review, February 28, 2019.

46   Andrew Riley, "Ostracism More Damaging than Bullying in the Workplace," The University of British Columbia, May 29, 2014.

47   Rik Kirkland et al., "Focusing on What Works for Workplace Diversity," McKinsey & Company, April 7, 2017.

48   Laura Sherbin et al., "Diversity Doesn't Stick Without Inclusion," Harvard Business Review, February 1, 2017.

49   Johana Bhuiyan et al., "Black and Brown Tech Workers Share Their Experiences of Racism on the Job." Los Angeles Times. June 24, 2020.

50   Matthew Lieberman et al., "The Pains and Pleasures of Social Life: a Social Cognitive Neuroscience Approach," Science, February 2009.

it's an issue for all of us. Belonging is something we need to get a better handle on, so we can learn how to turn things around when they go wrong.

Everyone wants to feel like they matter. Everyone wants to feel loved. These are fundamental needs. Secure relationships satisfy these needs and can lead to healthier, more productive, and more rewarding lives. When these needs go unmet, we suffer.[51]

Organizations will continue to need tough conversations around inclusion and connection. A company's productivity, resilience, and even its survival depends on its ability to make sure people feel supported and heard.[52]

Belonging allows employees to feel like they can be their real selves without fear of being excluded or diminished, and it has a major impact on performance and retention. Belonging looks like being recognized for your accomplishments, expressing your opinions freely, feeling comfortable being your true self at work, and feeling that the organization cares about your place in it.

INCLUSION AND BELONGING IN A DISTRIBUTED WORKFORCE

Leaders across all industries have to start reimagining what inclusion means in an increasingly distributed workforce.

---

51 Vivek Murthy, *Together: The Healing Power of Human Connection in a Sometimes Lonely World,* New York: Harper Wave, 2020.

52 George Serafeim, "Corporate Resilience and Response During COVID-19," State Street, April 2020.

Working from home has become a lot more common in response to COVID-19. This forced experiment of remote work offers us an unprecedented opportunity to integrate more inclusive habits with our remote workforces. As remote work moves from the "new normal" to the "next normal," the most forward-thinking leaders will incorporate new systems and values right now.

WHAT DOES REMOTE INCLUSION LOOK LIKE?

At the time of this writing, the American workforce has been dealing with the stresses of COVID-19 while also processing the impacts of racial injustice that have hit many employees very personally. Leaders across the country have emphasized the importance of community, both in and out of the office.

As we transition into remote work, we have the chance to supercharge sponsorship of underrepresented employees. What's the difference between a mentor and a sponsor? In simple terms, a mentor is someone who talks to you, and a sponsor is someone who talks about you. A mentor helps a less experienced person learn the ropes. A sponsor advocates for you when you're not around. They recommend you take part in the next big project or the next big meeting. They promote you when new leadership opportunities arise. As we move to increases in remote work, sponsorship becomes incredibly important, especially in hybrid situations where some employees work from home while others transition back to physical office spaces.

INCLUSION IS REMOTE SPONSORSHIP

A Bain & Company study showed that 43 percent of women aspired toward top management positions, versus 34 percent of men. Yet, this figure for women changed to 16 percent within two years, while there was no change for men. The drop for women didn't come from a lack of confidence or new family obligations but from a lack of belonging and support from supervisors, who were largely male.[53] Pulitzer Prize Winner Joanne Lipman sums it up well: "Women's mentors usually give them advice. But men's champions act as sponsors, with the power to get them promotions and new jobs. There's a world of difference between mentors and sponsors. And that's a crucial advantage for men."[54]

Sponsors can be career savers for remote employees. Being "out of sight, out of mind" can be a career crusher for remote employees. Sponsors help reverse that path by including remote employees in key conversations and advocating for them in the employee's absence.

INCLUSION MEANS ACCEPTING AND EMBRACING PEOPLE FROM DIFFERENT LOCATIONS

One of the most compelling perspectives I have read about inclusion in a remote workforce comes from Kevin Smith,

---

53   Julie Coffman and Bill Neuenfeldt, "Everyday Moments of Truth: Frontline Managers Are Key to Women's Career Aspirations," Bain & Company, June 17, 2014.

54   Joane Lipman, *That's What She Said: What Men Need to Know (and Women Need to Tell Them) About Working Together* New York: William Morrow, 2018.

Co-founder of remote startup Abstract.[55] Here was a Silicon Valley dream company that had intentionally bucked nearly every conventional Silicon Valley mold. There were no giant Abstract campuses, no endless office chatter, and no giant conference rooms named after astronauts or popular TV shows. In fact, the founders of Abstract believed that a traditional office was hardly required or even necessary. To that end, their company was primarily distributed, with no one tied to a particular physical location.

This lack of a physical "headquarters" sometimes gives people pause. They wonder how a distributed company can emulate an inclusive culture where people would feel like they were part of a larger community instead of a lone contributor sitting by their laptop at home.

I talked to Kevin in the summer of 2020 to learn more about his thoughts about how a remote workforce could be the key to improving inclusion and supporting local economies.

Kevin sees distributed workforces as change agents for inclusive cultures in the future. "It's a deeper discussion than just working from home versus working in an office," Kevin told me. "I've always wondered how you can scale kindness and happiness. In the midst of the chaos and the cacophony of the growth of (our) company, I would often ask that question. And I think remote work is a part of that."

---

55   Kevin Smith, "Why Remote Work is Inclusion Work," Abstract, July 10, 2019.

Kevin went on to talk about the importance of being open to allowing people to work from anywhere. First, the odds that all the best people for your organization will be scattered within a 10-mile radius of a central office location seems almost laughable, so for the sake of the organization, it makes sense to cast a wider net so you can hire the best people. Second, if scaling kindness and happiness is the goal, then it makes sense to support remote workers who can work in the location they want, near the communities they love, around people and experiences that help them thrive and make them happy.

Kevin told me about someone who had started working with the company in Silicon Valley to drive this point home. Partway through her time at Abstract, she said, "Well, I kind of want to move to New York. But before I do that, I actually want to go spend three months in Portugal and just kind of experience the culture there... but I can work the whole time."

And that is exactly what she did. The amazing thing? There was no disruption to her work at all. Many people didn't even realize she had left the country because the workflow and work product were fluid. She was able to weave her work and her life together and be her whole self at work. Remote inclusion happens when you realize that office spaces aren't magical. Respecting an employee's desire to work from a particular location and trusting that she will contribute value to the company, is what remote inclusion is all about.

In addition to individual accommodations, Kevin spent some time talking about the need for collective reflection when striving for an inclusive remote workforce, especially in the difficult situations where some employees are still in a traditional office setting while others are at home. It's not as easy as telling people to take their laptop home and then continuing with business as usual. A hybrid workforce can be tricky to manage and can put remote workers at a disadvantage.

Kevin gave an example of how Abstract has an office in the Bay area for people who want to work in the office. When they opened the new office, Abstract initially thought about implementing a traditional office space with conference rooms and TVs for video conferencing.

They discovered, though, that this wasn't the best route to inclusion for a remote team because it didn't create a level playing field for remote workers. Abstract talked to its people and made adjustments to its in-office experience. They also decided to host all of their meetings in the same way, which meant each individual signed in from a computer, whether or not they were at Abstract's physical locations. They logged in to meetings the same way. This unified the experience for everyone, so there was one working culture. Kevin and his team worked hard to ensure that no one group had different advantages over another. Management created a cohesive work style for everyone, which prevented anyone on the team from adopting a "me" versus "we" mindset. Kevin said the key is to remember that basic human dynamics, like feeling included, don't change just because the work's location does.

Having addressed inclusion within a remote company, Kevin continued. He spoke passionately about inclusion in a broader sense, one that transcended the organization. His idea of inclusion in a broader sense started with an analysis of the "Two Americas":

- Tech is where the future wealth lies. Kevin starts by talking about the idea of Two Americas, where life is different for those with privilege versus those living paycheck to paycheck. Working in the tech space, Kevin believes that the tech economy is the future of American wealth and opportunity. Based on the net worth of people like Jeff Bezos, Mark Zuckerberg, and Bill Gates, it would be hard to argue against him.
- Tech hubs are often in unaffordable locations. What areas do you think of when you hear the tech economy? Silicon Valley for sure, but also places like Seattle, New York City, and Los Angeles. What do all of these areas have in common? The cost of living is obscene, and it's borderline impossible to afford real estate.
- Remote work makes both inclusion and homeownership possible. Going back to the Two Americas idea, one of the differentiators between the "haves" and the "have nots" is homeownership, something Kevin reminds us creates stability and security for people.[56] Homeownership in expensive tech areas is difficult, if not impossible, for many underrepresented classes. By letting people work remotely, home ownership becomes an attainable goal for a lot more people.
- Remote work supports community and belonging. Kevin notes that being part of their local community helps keep their language, culture, and rituals intact for

---

56 William Rohe and Mark Lindblad, "Reexaming the Social Benefits of Homeownership after the Housing Crisis," April 2013.

underrepresented people. When we ask people to choose between their livelihood and their community, he says, we weaken both the individual and the community from which they are being separated.

Remote work could have a meaningful impact on the employee, their families, and their local communities. "What if, instead of asking people to leave their support system and come to a new place, we use remote work to bring the opportunity to that individual?" Kevin asked. In this case, the company becomes a vehicle for connecting people across cities, cultures, backgrounds, and abilities. Flexible and remote schedules allow people to invest time back into their families, neighborhoods, and communities. Employees can build stronger support systems in familiar areas, gain financial security through homeownership, and maintain connections to their local communities that are a foundational piece of holistic thriving and wellbeing.

Kevin's philosophy on remote workforces boils down to this: building a distributed workforce with remote workers is about way more than allowing people to set up an office at home. It's about promoting a sense of inclusion, community, and impact. Kevin takes the stance that working remotely is a means to an end. The "end" is honoring the whole person so they can thrive in their life no matter where they are while having access to wealth and opportunity that a tech economy amply offers. This circles back to Kevin's original question: how can we scale happiness and kindness? Though not easy, his answer is simple: The recent advancements of technology have offered an unprecedented opportunity to make distributed workforces possible. If we want to foster compassionate people who are part of compassionate communities, Kevin says, organizations need to do their part by utilizing every tool they can to foster inclusion, thriving, and wellbeing of its people.

Flexibility, like work-from-home options, can solve the problem of recruiting diverse candidates who might be great candidates but are unwilling to relocate. The key to making inclusion work is leading by example, whether you're in a high-rise office or at the desk near your kitchen table.

In sum, inclusion and belonging are the things that make diversity stick. Inclusion and belonging are about accepting, embracing, and celebrating people for who they are. Inclusion and belonging are about listening and learning. It's about the simplicity of caring about other people. Whether it's in person or remotely, inclusion and belonging are good for business. More importantly, they're the keys to building humanity in the workforce.

CHAPTER THREE

WHAT IS WELLBEING?

—

"If we try to secure the wellbeing of others, we will, at the same time, create the conditions for our own."

-THE FOURTEENTH DALAI LAMA[57]

"Chemotherapy felt like a vacation," Dina told me.

In a 2019 interview for my *Sweatours* wellbeing podcast, Dina Cataldo shared her personal journey with her wellbeing struggles. Dina had been a criminal prosecutor for over a decade, trying cases from burglary to homicide. She used to joke with other attorneys about how it would be nice to have a small accident – like being hit by a bus—just to get a break. She never thought her joke would manifest itself in real life.[58]

---

57 Daniel Goleman, *Destructive Emotions: A Scientific Dialogue with the Dalai Lama*, Bantam Books, 2003.

58 Anjali Bindra Patel, "'Chemo Seemed Like a Vacation': When Lawyers Hit a Breaking Point," September 23, 2019, in *SweaTours: Law Student Well Being* Podcast.

Dina received a breast cancer diagnosis at 29, while she was working 50-70 hours a week as a trial attorney. At first, she couldn't fathom making time for endless appointments—there was just too much she needed to do at work. However, she knew nothing would matter if she wasn't well enough to do it.

Dina listened to her doctor's urging to undergo chemotherapy treatments. Once the chemo was in full swing, Dina knew she needed to make a change when "chemo seemed like a vacation." Dina had been in a constant mental and emotional grind at work as a trial lawyer. Getting time away from work, no matter the reason, was a relief. During chemo, she thought, "if chemo is a vacation, then something needs to change. There's more to my life than just work."

The truth is that the hours we spend at work can't be separated from the hours we spend outside of it, especially with remote work blurring the lines between home life and work life. Many of us find ourselves in a repeating loop of pings, notifications, and deadlines. The average American will spend over 90,000 hours, or one third, of their life at work, and now that our workspaces are spilling over into our living spaces, feeling good and functioning well at work are critical components of a person's overall wellbeing.[59] Given that work impacts our wellbeing, and our wellbeing impacts an organization's success, it's in a company's best interest to support and promote wellbeing at work.[60]

---

59 "One Third of Your Life is Spent at Work," Gettysburg College, accessed August 9, 2020.

60 Alexis Keeman et al., "Employee Wellbeing: Evaluating a Wellbeing Intervention in Two Settings." *Frontiers in Psychology* 8 (April 2017).

Think of it like this: Imagine you own a car. Your engine looks good, and maybe your brakes are in good shape, but you don't have a steering wheel. Guess what? You're probably not getting to your destination. That leads to the next question, can we actually improve elements of our wellbeing? Of course, the answer is yes, and this can happen on both an individual and an organizational level. First, let's define wellbeing.

ELEMENTS OF WELLBEING

My first real foray into articulating wellbeing came after a visit to the Paul Duda Gallery, which is walking distance from my parents' house in Cleveland. Though I'm not much of an art connoisseur, there were some cool pieces in the window when I went to see my parents the prior Christmas, so I ventured inside.

One of the watercolor pieces instantly took me back to the 1980s when I had my first real exposure to art. When I was in second grade, I met this kid named Gary, a really good finger painter. Even as an eight-year-old, he did not doubt that he would one day become an art teacher. He had no plan B. He knew what he wanted, and there was no stopping him.

For some reason, this particular memory kept bubbling to the surface during my Cleveland trip. My curiosity finally got the better of me, so I looked Gary up on Facebook and messaged him. As it turned out, he indeed did grow up to become an art teacher. He was teaching at a local high school near Cleveland.

We spent some time catching up. He told me about his boyfriend. I talked about my kids. I mentioned that I was writing a book about wellbeing, diversity, and inclusion, and he asked what the word wellbeing even meant.

"What does the term wellbeing even mean?" he pressed. "It's one of those terms that's hard to define without actually using the word itself."

Gary's question was valid. Wellbeing can be a tricky term to define. Ask 20 people, and you'll get 20 different answers. Generally speaking, wellbeing at work includes feelings of satisfaction toward work. More specifically, wellbeing includes all aspects of working life, from the quality and safety of your environment, to how you feel about your work, environment, and level of belonging. Wellbeing at work refers to a subjective perception of general satisfaction with positive feelings toward work.

When people come to work, they bring their worries, sicknesses, and anxieties. We know that when our workforce is healthy, we have more energy to do our jobs better. The company, in turn, benefits by increased engagement, productivity, and health care savings.

Talking to Gary, it became clear that he was in a caring and authentic work environment. The attrition rate was low. The connectivity tissue of the school seemed strong. The impact of a compassionate school culture seemed clear: he was content.

Sure, he had some unpleasant elements to his job (periodic lack of supplies, students who didn't take the class seriously), but Gary was engaged with his work and his colleagues, and even with some students. He said that he wanted to be remembered as someone who loved creating art and loved teaching it. After Gary and I chatted, he concluded that his level of wellbeing was pretty high. He loved his job, loved his colleagues, and enjoyed his students' presence, and he felt his work was purposeful.

So how can the rest of us get to Gary's level of wellbeing? We can start by breaking down the term and classifying its elements. There are countless ways to break down elements of wellbeing, but I like a combination of components proposed by the Centers for Disease Control and Prevention and the American Bar Association:

1. Emotional/mental wellbeing. Emotional/mental wellbeing is about our ability to accept and understand ourselves to best deal with the challenges of our personal and work lives. It's about being resilient, recognizing and channeling our frustration, hope, fear, anger, stress, and anxieties.

2. Spiritual wellbeing. Spiritual wellbeing links to emotional wellbeing and includes developing a sense of purpose of meaning both in and out of work. It's about being fulfilled by what we do and about having our actions match our values.

3. Occupational wellbeing. Occupational wellbeing is about maximizing our satisfaction at work. It's about being able to bring our whole selves to work (not having to pretend to be someone we're not), and it's about being able to

be productive and comfortable. Occupational wellbeing also includes things like ergonomic chairs, healthy food options, and smoke-free offices.[61]

4. Financial wellbeing. A close cousin to occupational wellbeing is financial security. Though we all stress about our finances from time to time, a person with a strong sense of financial wellbeing doesn't have a persistent worry about outstanding bills, mounting debt, or job security.

5. Intellectual wellbeing. The American Bar Association defines intellectual wellbeing as continuous learning and pursuit of creative or intellectually challenging activities that foster ongoing development.[62]

6. Physical wellbeing. Physical wellbeing is all about taking proper care of our bodies to function at an optimal level. It includes things like exercise, nutrition, diet, and sleep.

7. Social wellbeing. Social wellbeing is about developing a connection, belonging, and becoming part of a compassionate community. Someone with a strong sense of social wellbeing has a support system to lean on and a network of people there to listen.

These elements of wellbeing impact everything from our job performance to our longevity at our company.

To address these elements of wellbeing, we need to combine three wellbeing interventions: tertiary, secondary, and primary. Some interventions point to individual responsibility, while other interventions focus on an organization's role.

---

61 "Wellbeing Concepts," Centers for Disease Control and Prevention, accessed August 3, 2020.

62 Bree Buchanan et al., "The Path to Lawyer Well-being," American Bar, August 14, 2017.

TERTIARY WELLBEING INTERVENTIONS

Tertiary wellbeing aims to rehabilitate employees who are already suffering due to various stressors and conditions. It's about trying to improve your own quality of life and reduce the symptoms of a disease or condition that you already have. It puts the responsibility on you to change your existing circumstances and conditions. In a medical context, it's about trying to prevent a bad thing from getting worse.[63]

Mike Yeung is an example of someone who used tertiary interventions to improve his wellbeing. I first learned about Mike a couple of years ago when my kids and I started an inter-generational Esports program. (Esports is a form of sport competition using video games. It usually takes the form of organized multiplayer video game competitions, either individually or as teams. Another definition? Esports is sports with an "E" for electronic.)

As the kids and I ramped up our program, we met a lot of Esports athletes and had a lot of conversations about their stressors, their lifestyles, and their fears. In my talks with all these younger Esports athletes, I heard about Mike Yeung, who played League of Legends (LoL stands for League of Legends here, not laugh out loud) since season one, reaching challenger rank during season three while only 13 years old. Mike absolutely electrified the League of

---

63   Ryan Wolf, "Wellbeing by Generation: Where Some Thrive, Others Struggle," Gallup, November 8, 2019.

Legends Championship Series Arena week after week. Huge crowds would scream his name: the chants were completely deafening.[64]

Bad eating habits, chronic stress, and long hours started taking their toll, and soon, Mike suffered a downslide. The self-imposed pressure built up and found no release. He wasn't alone. A lot of young Esports athletes felt similarly. One Esports athlete recently told me: "*I noticed that I started to sacrifice my personal health to be online a lot. A lot of people get into those ruts thinking, 'I'm just going to play. ... I'm not going to eat. I've got a bag of chips right here.'*"

Tertiary interventions for many Esports athletes included regular doctor appointments for the rehabilitation of chronic pain and injuries, individualized dietician consultations, and counseling to address the root cause of their stress. With tertiary wellbeing, the impetus is on the individual to seek help to improve their own wellbeing.

SECONDARY WELLBEING INTERVENTIONS

Secondary wellbeing interventions are in the next rung of interventions: this is when the organization takes active steps to cope with existing conditions or prevents an existing problem from becoming chronic or acute. Secondary interventions include things like mindfulness coaching, time management seminars, or resilience training.

---

64   Miles Yim, "Self-Imposed Pressure, Outside Criticism Nearly Crushed a 'League of Legends' Phenom. Now He's Back," The Washington Post, July 11, 2019.

There is real value in secondary wellbeing interventions because it helps shift our mindset and improve our wellbeing. The nice thing about secondary intervention training is that it doesn't have to occur in a conference room or on a webinar. Some of the best secondary interventions are the ones we see playing out in real life.

One real-life example of a secondary intervention comes from my friend, entrepreneur Jesse Itzler. Jesse is an owner of the Atlanta Hawks, a two-time bestselling author, Co-founder of Marquis Jets, and partner in numerous consumer companies. He juggles all this while being a dad to four kids and husband to the billionaire owner of Spanx, Sara Blakely.

All of his business accolades are impressive, but that's not what makes him unique: his resilience and ability to vicariously educate and inspire others is what makes him so memorable.

In the fall of 2019, Jesse decided that he would take part in a race called the Last Man Standing Ultramarathon. The goal was to run a 4.2-mile rough terrain loop every hour. People ran the same loop over and over. Ultimately in this race, one man (athlete) is left standing.

On race day, I followed the race from the comfort of my couch and saw that Jesse, a middle-aged man in his 50s, had run over 46 miles in 11 hours. He looked pretty spent, if I'm honest. Based on his appearance, I assumed that he was about to bow out. I was surprised when I checked in again at hour 14 and saw that Jesse was still running. Still running at hour 15. Still running at hour 16. Still running at hours 17, 18, and 19.

By hour 19, he was running in the pitch dark with a broken headlamp. He looked like his bones would detach from his frame, like those Halloween skeletons that blow apart on a windy Halloween night. And something else stood out: his big toe. The long-distance running had done a number on his feet. I can best describe his toe as... mangled. His toe looked like someone had removed it, put it in a blender, and then decided to place it back on his foot. It was a bloody mess. Yet, he went on running. And running some more.

In the end, Jesse timed out at 80 miles and 20 hours. To me, even *driving* a 4.2-mile loop for 20 hours sounds absolutely miserable, but here was this 51-year-old man who ran 80 miles (most of it in pitch dark conditions) coming in a stunning 5th place out of all the runners there.

Jesse's secondary wellbeing intervention isn't about working past your breaking point. Rather, it's about the power of resilience and connection. When trying to break down the source of his drive, he pointed to one thing: connection. "My favorite part of the race was hugging my friends and my wife when I came out of the tent before every lap. I'm still high off all the love," Jesse said.

It became clear that Jesse's performance wasn't ultimately about his endurance. It was about his resilience. The two terms aren't interchangeable. Confusing these terms can get us into trouble.

Endurance is a short view game. "Stay at the office all night, every night, until you get this brief done" is endurance. It might work in the short term, but it's not sustainable.

Resilience, on the other hand, is a long game. Resilience is about taking care of yourself mentally, physically, spiritually, and socially so you can function at your highest level in the long run. It consists of 3 elements:

1. <u>Connection</u>. Resilience is about connection. It seems like a big part of what kept Jesse running was his family and friends' support. Those connections matter. They are critical to our wellbeing. They strengthen our resolve.
2. <u>Positive Outcomes in the Light of Improbability and Trauma</u>. In my objective analysis, a 51-year-old man probably wouldn't be expected to finish in the top 5 of a grueling race. Still, Jesse adapted to trauma (sore legs, blurry vision during the race, and a nasty toe injury, just to name the physical trauma elements).
3. <u>Competence During Stressful Times; Using Challenges for Growth</u>. Running through the entire night with a broken headlamp sounds like the prelude to a Netflix horror movie, so let's all agree that Jesse's race qualifies as a stressful time. Still, he nonetheless showed competence through its duration, just by staying in it.

Jesse will surely be using the life lessons from his race for sustained personal growth in the future. I'm sure every time he looks down at his mangled toe, he will be reminded of everything he did to earn that (visually memorable) souvenir.

The secondary wellbeing takeaway from Jesse's race is this: work will be tough. Stressful days, though hopefully infrequent, will happen. When they do, we can lean into our resilience, something Clinical Psychologist Rick Hanson defines as "the thing that keeps us on a relatively even keel when the waves come. It's the thing that helps you recover when you get knocked down. Resilience is a combination of grit, compassion, gratitude, agility, and emotional intelligence, and it's the thing that helps us cope so we can maintain a fundamental sense of wellbeing. Resilience is something that can be cultivated by dealing with the bad, turning to the good, and internalizing the good."[65]

Jesse's secondary intervention came in the form of real-life experiences, with the lesson being this: resilience, whether it's an ultramarathon race or a challenging time at work, can be cultivated through connection. We shouldn't feel the need to apologize for prioritizing our loved ones. They are often the power source that help us recharge and become our best selves. Our connections build resilience. So, during those tough times, we can weather the storm with our best feet forward, mangled toes and all.

PRIMARY WELLBEING INTERVENTIONS

The third and final type of wellbeing intervention is primary. Primary interventions look at the big issues from a macro level. Primary interventions are all about organizational wide culture and structural shifts. Implementing an effective primary intervention is no easy feat. All these definitions and classifications can get a bit murky and technical, but this social media post effectively illustrates both primary interventions and resistances to implementing them:

---

65   Miles Yim, "Self-Imposed Pressure, Outside Criticism Nearly Crushed a 'League of Legends' Phenom. Now He's Back," The Washington Post, July 11, 2019.

Company: We'd like to promote mental health in the workplace. We care about the team's wellbeing.

Employee: How about hiring more people so we feel less pressure and increasing our pay so we can deal with the spiraling costs of living so we're not as stressed out?

Company: LOL. Not like that. Let's try yoga.[66]

Unlike this social media post, primary interventions are not about treating symptoms. They are about attacking the problems that are eroding wellbeing. Primary interventions focus on the organization and seek to reduce or even eliminate various stressors. One of the biggest stressors at work comes from a lack of emotional wellbeing, which is related to a low sense of social wellbeing at work. People want to feel respected, valued, heard, and connected at work, but sadly, this is often where things start to unravel.

Even though belonging was covered in the inclusion chapter, it also needs a shout-out here. Belongingness is often overlooked at work because we're so focused on our goals that we don't pay enough attention to how those around us feel. A study by professors at UCLA found that threats to belonging result in experiences similar to physical pain. And that's just the beginning. Other studies have shown that not belonging or feeling a lack of acceptance can also lead to

---

66   Patrick Patid, Twitter, March 20, 2019.

depression, reduced problem-solving skills, and a decrease in job effectiveness.[67]

How can organizations work on broad primary interventions, particularly those related to emotional and social wellbeing? These questions have been researched extensively by the United Kingdom's Department of Health, which, among other things, suggests a continuous improvement approach to the following psychosocial job factors: effort-reward balance, decision latitude, psychological demands, and social support.[68]

What does the continuous improvement approach look like in action? We may not need to look any further than our underwear drawers to find out.

SARA BLAKELY'S USE OF PSYCHOSOCIAL JOB FACTORS

1. Psychosocial Factor 1: Effort/Reward Balance

"If you can create a culture where your employees are not terrified to fail or make a mistake, then they're going to be highly productive and more innovative."

-SARA BLAKELY[69]

---

67   Matthew Lieberman and Naomi I. Eisenberger, "The Pains and Pleasures of Social Life: A Social Cognitive Neuroscience Approach," *Science* 323, no. 5916, (February 2009): 890-91.

68   Sarah Brand et al., "Whole-System Approaches to Improving the Health and Wellbeing of Healthcare Workers: A Systematic Review." *PLoS One* 12, no. 12 (December 2017).

69   Blaie Briody, "Sara Blakely: Start Small, Think Big, Scale Fast." Stanford Graduate School of Business. June 21, 2018.

Sara Blakely is the billionaire founder and owner of shapewear brand Spanx, which sells undergarments, leggings, swimwear, and maternity wear in 65 countries. She is also married to Jesse, the resilient guy with the mangled toe. She was born in Clearwater, Florida, in 1971. As a child, her dad would use dinnertime to ask her and her brother, "What did you fail at this week?" After each child talked about their various failed encounters, their dad would proudly encourage them to keep trying and keep failing.[70]

Sara's childhood "fail forward" dinner tradition now permeates the culture at Spanx. At Spanx, failure comes from *not* trying versus the outcome. Hosong Na, a senior photo editor at Spanx, says, "We're encouraged to experiment with new ways of doing things... it's great because Spanx encourages us to fail. You learn from your failures, and I fail all the time!"[71]

Part of our emotional and mental wellbeing at work comes from the freedom of knowing that we won't be reprimanded for new ways of thinking, executing, and approaching issues. Spanx's encouragement rewards the effort, not the outcome, which is a key component to both mental and occupational wellbeing at work. In other words, it's commending someone for studying and learning, not the grade.

70 Kristen Bareman, "How I Get It Done: Sara Blakely of Spanx." The Cut. June 26, 2018.

71] Field, Hayden. "What It's Like Inside Spanx Headquarters." Entrepreneur. November 15, 2019.

2. Psychosocial Factor 2: Decision Latitude

Decision latitude is about someone's potential control over their tasks and actions at work. Basically, it's about conveying the message: "You can do this."

At Spanx, Sara wanted to avoid mission drift, knowing that it was important for the company culture to reflect its mission: empowerment. To that end, employees are encouraged to work on projects outside their departments, and the company designs specific activities to inspire courage in decision making. Spanx created a program called Be Bold Bootcamp to show that it's not just a tag line to take risks and try new things; it's part of their ethos. As part of Be Bold, employees learn to take risks through getting involved with the training you might not find at other organizations: a stint at a comedy club or a debate tournament at a law school is not out of the norm at Spanx.

Regarding the company's mission to embrace decision latitude, Gabrielle Baker, an e-commerce associate at Spanx, stated: "As part of our year-round Be Bold program, every quarter the staff is trained on new skills. We've had debate tournaments and negotiation training, but my favorite was last year's comedy boot camp. We went to Atlanta's Punchline Comedy Club, and everyone got up on stage to perform. It was a great way to stretch and grow."[72]

Alie Ferst, director of international accounts, had this to say: "You're encouraged to raise your hand and say, 'I want to be a part of that.' Before we opened our London office, I was on

---

72 Ibid.

the sales team, but I asked for a bigger role and to become more involved in the opening of the new London office... and now my role covers all international markets."[73]

Decision latitude gives workers the freedom to innovate, create, and invest in their company's culture in a meaningful way. It's a powerful way to promote wellbeing from a mental, occupational, and social perspective.

3. Psychosocial Factor 3: Psychological Demands (Parental Leave, Aging Parents, and Other Personal Needs)

In addition to effort-reward balance and decision latitude, psychological demands are an important factor when implementing primary wellbeing interventions with mental, emotional, and occupational wellbeing. How hard are you being asked to work? Are late nights and weekends a usual occurrence? Are parental leave policies adequately supporting your needs? Do you have the support you need to accomplish your tasks and reach your goals? How are your personal extra-job considerations influencing your health, work performance, and job satisfaction?

To address some of these questions on a deeper level, Spanx launched its "Made of More" Initiative in 2019. Regarding the intent of the initiative, Sara stated:

"Spanx is what it is because of every one of you. You make the culture. You make the company. You make the products that make the difference in the world. but you're so much more than what you are at Spanx... you're also spouses, you're

---

73   Ibid.

parents, you're sisters, you're brothers, and that's what Made of More celebrates."[74]

About the working environment as a working parent, Courtney Perkins, a sales associate, said: "Spanx was my first job after spending 12 years as a stay-at-home mom. It was so foreign to think about being in a corporate environment again. But every time I got on the elevator with people I didn't recognize, someone reached out to me and said, 'I don't recognize you. Are you new? Welcome to Spanx!"[75]

Other employees pointed to the generous benefit plans, the half days on Fridays, and generous parental leave policies. All of these factors point to concerted attention being paid to the lives people lead outside of work, as well as the ones they bring to the office.

Incremental improvements across all facets of wellbeing happen when companies take psychological factors into account. No company is perfect, including Spanx, but one thing seems clear: the company cares about its people and is willing to make an effort to be an employer of choice.

4. Psychosocial Factor 4: Social Support

One of the most important things we can give our employees is our attention. The most basic human need is to be understood. We need to hear what our employees are really telling us. We need to know them and see what makes them tick. We need to allow them to be vulnerable and be vulnerable right

---

74   Instagram, 2019 Spanx Page Stories.
75   Field, Hayden. "What It's Like Inside Spanx Headquarters." Entrepreneur. November 15, 2019.

back. We need to share a sense of purpose and belonging. We need to inspire each other, learn from one another, and be there for each other.

We often assume that people are unstressed because they seem competent and produce great, or at least acceptable, work products. But assumptions can have us connecting dots that aren't there and painting pictures that don't exist. We may assume that we are doing enough to champion wellbeing, even if we aren't.

Work culture is often at the root of these issues. Companies, and the people who work for them, sink or swim based on workplace culture. We can't talk about improving employee wellbeing without analyzing a company's culture.

In 2019, I had the opportunity to visit the Spanx corporate headquarters in Atlanta. When I arrived, the first thing I noticed was the laid-back atmosphere. The walls were cheery. The space was inviting. The conference rooms had quirky names. I walked past a meeting space and asked myself out loud, "Wait, was that conference room really called Booby Trap?" An employee who was walking past heard me and smiled. She introduced herself and asked if I was new, and she told me about some of the other conference rooms: Brallywood and Shape Shack were a couple of the rooms nearby.

I was curious whether the laid-back environment matched the employee sentiment, so I casually asked a few employees about their experience. One person talked about the great health insurance, while another told me how the company was very supportive of taking time to tend to family obligations. (Sara is a mom to 4 young kids, so that could play into the organization's family-friendly culture.)

When I met Sara in person, she said she liked my outfit (I was wearing Spanx) and promptly had her team lead me to a mini photoshoot, which they later posted on social media. It might be relevant to note that I am no Instagram model. I am a regular mom with a regular life. That's part of the magic behind the Spanx brand: there is no set ideal of beauty or success. Everyone is embraced not despite their unique backgrounds, ages, perspectives, and ideas, but because of them.

People from all departments and backgrounds are in regular contact with one another, celebrating each other's achievements, whether it's a big contract or the simple fact that the kids got to school on time. That type of micro and macro support has a positive correlative impact on a person's confidence and, ultimately, on their wellbeing.

My personal takeaway from my time at Spanx HQ was that its culture matched its clothing: supportive, reliable, comfortable, and empowering.

REMOTE WELLBEING

As we transition into an increasingly remote workforce, the importance of wellbeing for both in and out-of-office employees can't be overstated. Before the COVID-19 pandemic, the US workforce had already seen a huge uptick in partial or fully remote employees, to the tune of nearly 43 percent of

US workers, according to Gallup's "State of the American Workplace" report.[76]

As more and more companies transition to a remote workforce, individuals will need to take extra care to implement tertiary interventions as needed, whether it's a session with a counselor or regular doctor visits for chronic pain. Managers will need to maintain relationships, build resilience for their teams, and support and engage their remote team members fully. Leaders at the top will have to take a detailed overview of their organization and look at factors like social support, psychological needs, decision latitude, and effort/performance metrics. They will also need to start having some uncomfortable conversations about improving workplace wellbeing by addressing systemic and cultural issues that may negatively impact wellbeing. These conversations can lead to improved processes and policies that will positively impact the wellbeing of the organization's most important asset: its people.

So here is the takeaway on wellbeing: the hard part is not getting employers to care. Many of them already want improved wellbeing for their employees.

The problem is their inability or unwillingness to listen to what employees really need. In many of my client meetings, I ask employers if they ever sat down with their employees to learn about their day-to-day life, both in and out of work. The resounding answer is "no." This begs the question: how can we help people if we don't even truly know who they are?

---

76 "State of the American Workplace," Gallup, 2017.

Think about it. A doctor doesn't toss prefabricated prescription plans at her patients without speaking to them first. To treat her patients, she first diagnoses them. And to diagnose, she first listens.

Listening is how we diagnose the state of our people's well-being. An annual survey is *not* listening. Tossing employees a code for a free meditation app and then leaving their well-being to fate is *not* listening.

When you really listen to your employees, you might learn that they don't want high-end dinners at the office: they want to be appreciated for their efforts.

When you listen to your employees, you might learn that they don't want premium espresso machines in every office: they want broader decision latitude.

When you listen to your employees, you might learn that they don't want more tech gadgets: they want the chance to power down at night.

In 1938, researchers at Harvard University started studying 268 sophomores to examine a question that we have all have wondered: what is the secret to happiness and long life? After almost 80 years of research, the answer for both, they found, was easy: relationships.[77] By making a habit of listening, we can get to know our people and form a culture that people want to join.

---

77   Liz Mineo, "Good Genes are Nice, but Joy is Better: Harvard Study, Almost 80 Years Old, Has Proved That Embracing Community Helps Us Live Longer, and Be Happier," The Harvard Gazette, April 11, 2017.

CHAPTER FOUR

CROSSROADS BETWEEN DIVERSITY, INCLUSION, AND WELLBEING

"People will forget what you said, people will forget what you did, but people will never forget how you made them feel."
                                                    - MAYA ANGELOU[78]

Years ago, when I was a new associate, I attended a professional networking event. For Diversity Day, we were asked to bring, wear, or share any part of our culture of which we were proud.

I went all out. On Diversity Day, I wore a neon yellow lehenga (think Indian prom gown), and I had brought enough Indian food to feed an army. The day was still in its early hours, but

---

78   Carmine Gallo, "The Maya Angelou Quote That Will Radically Improve Your Business," Forbes, May 31, 2014.

the spicy scent of *paneer tikka masala* was wafting through the air and making me hungry for lunch. I walked into the event that morning feeling pretty excited and empowered.

As I stepped out of the elevator, I peered over at the banner hanging on the side of the reception desk that read: "Diversity—Embrace It. Accept It." The sign threw me off a bit because I couldn't quite understand the intent—there seemed to be a wide expanse between embracing something and merely accepting it. I was so preoccupied with dissecting the meaning of the sign that I didn't immediately notice that everyone around me was dressed as if it were just a regular day. No one looked any different than they ever had. Suddenly, I felt like there was a spotlight shining on me. The lights in the lobby seemed unusually bright; I could feel tiny beads of sweat trickling down my neck. My face felt like it was on fire. The food bags I had lugged in suddenly seemed insurmountably heavy; as I leaned over to set my *India House* bags down, my bangles clanged loudly against each other, like I had mini cymbals banging on my wrist.

"Oh my gosh, Anjali, your outfit is gorgeous," my friend stammered awkwardly, trying to mask his shock. My head felt like a stack of bricks, too heavy to lift. All I could see in my peripheral vision were multiple pairs of black pant legs, the crook handle of an umbrella, and someone's designer Gucci socks. I wanted the floor to open up and swallow me.

I finally lifted my head and peered around the room. This was the first time I felt the impact of being the only female in the group. The normality around me felt less like a door to let me in and more like a wall to keep me out. All the guys had apparently emailed each other the night before and decided that participating in Diversity Day was too much trouble. Still, I was inadvertently left off the thread.

Now, I want to stop and say that I got many very respectful comments and questions that day. I definitely felt acknowledgment of my culture, but I have to tell you, I also felt like such an outsider. I contemplated taking a cab home to change my clothes. I couldn't leave that event fast enough. The group of guys in my group seemed genuinely respectful toward my culture, and any omission of me off their email thread seemed truly inadvertent.

So, if everyone was treating me nicely, why did everything still feel so wrong? Why was my head still throbbing? Why was my heart still pounding? Why was I getting cold sweats all day?

Could my level of inclusion have a direct impact on my wellbeing? Exactly how do diversity, inclusion, and wellbeing blend into one another?

INCLUSIVE WORKPLACES FOSTER WELLBEING

Feeling comfortable with being yourself at work (or at work-related events) might seem like a fuzzy goal, but it's a critical element to wellbeing.[79]

Our cultural backgrounds and other identifiers are a fundamental part of who we are and determine how comfortable

---

79 Adam Vaccaro, "Why Letting Employees Be Themselves Is So Darn Good for Business," Inc, January 6, 2014.

and effective we will be at work. Are we allowed to be our real selves, or do we feel pressured to "mask"? Does a mom feel like she has to take the pictures of her kids off her desk anytime leadership is nearby? Does a millennial struggling with mental illness have to use vacation days so he doesn't have to disclose that he is getting therapy? What about a gay woman who is reluctant to bring her partner to a work event? Is there a cost to all this covering? Yes, we often pay the price through reduced wellbeing. It's not just traditionally marginalized groups that pay. A study by Deloitte and NYU Professor Kenji Yoshino reports that 94 percent of racial minorities cover at work, and even 45 percent of straight white men hide parts of who they are.

Covering up who you are on a daily basis comes at a cost, the study concludes. It takes time and energy and is psychologically exhausting. Of those people who mask their identities, the Deloitte study found that between 60-66 percent say that "masking" is somewhat to extremely detrimental to their health.[80]

The news isn't all dire, though. When organizations prioritize inclusion by supporting work/life integration, supporting personal achievements, and encouraging a sense of community, our wellbeing and job satisfaction surge. Workers in inclusive teams are nineteen times more likely to be very satisfied with their job than non-inclusive teams.[81]

---

80 Christie Smith and Kenji Yoshino, "Uncovering Talent: A new model of inclusion," Deloitte, 2019.

81 Felicity Menzies, "How Does Employee Well-Being Link to Diversity and Inclusion?" Linkedin. September 5, 2018.

Inclusive workplaces lead to decreases in harassment, discrimination, and prejudice. Inclusivity makes us feel good, mentally, physically, and emotionally.[82]

Who wouldn't want that?

WELLBEING FOSTERS INCLUSIVE WORKPLACES

Inclusion can definitely impact our wellbeing, but the reverse is true too.

How patient are you toward other people when you haven't slept all week? How attentive are you to someone else's circumstances when you are experiencing debilitating pain? How collaborative are you toward your teammates when experiencing burnout symptoms like lack of energy or impaired concentration?

Let's tackle one specific element that impacts our wellbeing: stress. Research shows that stress can cause well-intentioned leaders to resort to bias and exclusion.[83] 83 percent of US workers suffer from work-related stress. Stress causes over a million people to miss work every day, and it costs American businesses about $300 billion a year as a result.[84] When we are stressed, we often feel pressed for time, so instead of letting a mentee figure out how to solve a problem,

---

82   Tchiki Davis, "What Is Well-Being? Definition, Types, and Well-Being Skills." Psychology Today. January 2, 2019.

83   Ethel Mickey et al., "10 Small Steps for Department Chairs to Foster Inclusion." Inside Higher Ed. June 5, 2020.

84   Milja Milenkovic, "42 Worrying Workplace Stress Statistics." The American Institute of Stress. September 23, 2019.

we do it for them because we don't have the patience to wait. We take shortcuts, and we rely on stereotypes to guide our responses.[85] Stress also increases our allostatic load—it's the "wear and tear" our bodies experience when exposed to stress, and it's associated with cardiovascular disease and diabetes.[86]

Another extremely important source of stress sometimes occurs outside of work but always blends into it: racism induced stress. In the past several years, there's been an increasing push by psychologists and psychiatrists to identify stress and trauma caused by racism, specifically the impact of racism on Black people's mental health.[87]

Not surprisingly, research has shown a strong link between racism, anxiety, post-traumatic stress disorder, and depression. In a July 2020 Wall Street Journal article, associate professor Sarah Y. Vinson stated: "If you are not thinking about societal, structural racism when it comes to Black mental health, you are missing a big part of it."[88]

Dr. Robert Carter, psychologist and developer of the "Race-Based Traumatic Stress Symptom Scale," describes race-based stress and trauma as an injury, not a disorder, meaning

85 Zawisza, Magdalena. "The Terrifying power of stereotypes—and how to deal with them." The Conversation. August 28, 2018.

86 David R. William, "Why Discrimination Is a Health Issue." Robert Wood Johnson Foundation. October 24, 2017.

87 Ray A. Smith, "For Some Black Americans, Therapy Is Gradually Losing Its Stigma." The Wall Street Journal. July 13, 2020.

88 bid.

that something was done to you, something did not develop within you.[89]

Regardless of where the race-based stress and trauma stemmed from, it's incumbent on every employer to recognize and address the impact racism has on its employees. It's not a political issue, it's a human issue, and as such, it's on you, the employer, to do something to help because your employee's wellbeing depends on it.

With the proper timing, attention, and compassion to understand each employee's whole self, it's possible to reduce workplace stress. What happens when we reduce workplace stress? We get employees who are more likely to listen, collaborate, communicate, and stay.[90]

INCLUSION IN WELLBEING
We covered how inclusion leads to wellbeing and how wellbeing leads to inclusion, but we also need to take a second to consider how we need inclusion IN wellbeing. Companies offering a wellbeing program need to think about the provisions of the programs and each element's accessibility and functionality.

- Have you thought about the various ages of your employees?

---

89 R.T. Carter et al., R. T., "Relationships Between Trauma Symptoms and Race-Based Traumatic Stress," *Traumatology*, 26(1), 11–18, 2020.
90 "Work-Related Stress." Better Health Channel. Accessed May 31, 2012.

- Have you considered how some physical wellbeing program components can be modified to include varying ranges of ability?
- If you are implementing a new healthy food catering service in your company, have you considered various food allergies or religious food restrictions? When building out a wellbeing program, it's important to consider the types of people you are catering to and their various backgrounds, perspectives, limitations, and challenges.

DIVERSITY IN WELLBEING

Diversity at work is great, but we also need a diverse approach to wellbeing, which is not "one size fits all." Consider the following:

- Strokes kill four times the number of 35 to 54-year-old Black Americans than whites.[91]
- Lesbian and bisexuals have higher rates of breast cancer versus heterosexuals.[92]
- Systemic lupus is two to three times more common among African Americans than whites. It's also more common for Latinx, Asian, and Native Americans.[93]

The list goes on: Millennials are at risk for loneliness and depression. Gen X'ers are at risk for burnout. Older workers

---

91   Hooman Kamel, "African American Patients Have Higher Risk of Stroke Recurrence Compared with White Patients." Weill Cornell Medicine. February 24, 2020.

92   Catherine Meads and David Moore, "Breast Cancer in Lesbians and Bisexual Women: Systematic Review of Incidence, Prevalence and Risk Studies." *BMC Public Health* 13, (December 2013): 1127.

93   "Lupus Facts and Statistics." National Resource Center on Lupus. Last modified October 6, 2016.

are at risk for chronic disease. Disabled workers need customized and accessible care.[94]

In a perfect world, every wellbeing program would be individually customized, like a tailor-made outfit. Since that is an unattainable goal for most companies, they need to take time to understand the demographics of who is working with them to best account for health concerns faced by different age groups, genders, races, ethnicities, and backgrounds. Are particular groups susceptible to mental health challenges like loneliness, depression, or anxiety? Are certain groups at an increased risk for cancer? Would a sizeable group of employees benefit from fertility treatments? Could certain groups benefit from financial wellbeing training related to paying off student loans, saving for children's college funds, or preparing for retirement?

The bottom line is that regardless of our age, gender, or ethnicity, we all share the basic human needs to connect deeply with others, feel loved, and matter. Who is at your company? Who are the people outside the role they fulfill at work? What do they need? How can you help? Asking these questions is what humanity at work is all about.

---

94 Hillary Hoffower, "The 'Loneliest Generation' Gets Lonelier: How Millennials are Dealing with the Anxieties of Isolation and the Uncertainties of Life After Quarantine." Business Insider. May 31, 2020.

PART TWO

THE "WHYS" OF DIVERSITY, INCLUSION, AND WELLBEING

CHAPTER FIVE

WHY DOES DIVERSITY MATTER?

———

"To celebrate diversity but to ignore disparity is hypocrisy."

- PASTOR STEVEN FURTICK[95]

As a lawyer, it's in my nature to defend my actions, even when they're questionable.

There have been a few times, though, where I have been an unequivocal and indefensible jerk.

One of those times happened a couple of decades ago. I had just graduated from law school and moved to the Lincoln Park area of Chicago. This was a fresh start for me: I was in a new city with a new roommate, ready to start a new job and meet new people.

---

95   Steven Furtick, "Become the Bridge," May 31, 2020, video, 1:07:20.

It wasn't long before I started getting to know a guy in my neighborhood. Let's call him Bill because, well, that's his actual name. At first, Bill was just my evening jogging partner, but it wasn't long before Bill went from workout buddy to real friend. After showing impressive resilience through multiple rounds of unprovoked attacks from my calico cat, he went from casual friend to someone I started to really care about. And that's when the problem started.

Let me back up a bit and explain. Growing up, I was raised primarily in an Indian community that worked hard to preserve its traditions, customs, food, and ideologies. Many of my better attributes stemmed from that upbringing. But I also carried some misguided notions in my head, one of them revolving around the "biodata" mindset. A biodata is basically a dating/marriage résumé, a tool to assess someone's potential compatibility. On its surface, the concept of a biodata isn't too problematic because regardless of what we call it, we all have a screening process of some sort to decide who stays in our lives and who doesn't.

So, it wasn't the idea of a biodata itself that now seems misguided, but the criteria we often screened for, with skin color at the top of that list. The biodata game was a tricky one because you wanted to be brown but not *too* brown. Fair skin was a huge asset. But being white? That was grounds for disqualification.

The more I grew to like Bill, the more I started to worry. "How is this going to play out at home? What if things actually get serious between us? Will I be disowned? What will people think? What will *he* think?"

Earlier in this book, I shared the story of TV host Hasan Minhaj and how he wasn't "good enough" to go to prom with a white girl. My life played out much like Hasan Minhaj's, except in reverse. The truth was that Bill would be just as "out of place" in our family photo album as Hasan would have been in his white high school girlfriend's pictures. Another truth? I felt too paralyzed to address the situation head-on. What would my parents say? And exactly how does a 24-year-old approach the topic of racial bias with someone they like? Is there a good way to tell someone you're judging them based on how quickly they burn in the sun?

The evidence that he cared for me was circumstantial. He showed up when I called because I was stressed about taking the bar exam. He took me to Tom Petty concerts. He was nice to my friends. He fed my cat while I was out of town. (That last one carried some weight because everyone *despised* my cat.)

But I still didn't feel confident about confronting my parents and was terrified of being humiliated, hurt, or both. Most people would know that having an open and honest conversation would be the right approach, but that just wasn't how I rolled. Vulnerability did not come easily to me, so, in the end, I went with the safest option: I torched the relationship.

I sometimes look back and wonder: did my actions make me racist? Was I any better than Hasan Minhaj's girlfriend? How is being an Indian who judges someone strictly because he is White any better than what Hasan experienced? Isn't it just the same problem in reverse?

Here's the thing: I judged a guy because I was biased. I'm still biased, just about other things now. You're biased too. We all are. Having biases doesn't make us bad people. Still, it does mean that we can hurt one another because of perceived and actual differences related to race, color, age, ethnicity, language, and a myriad of other factors. That's what makes diversity so valuable: it's the exposure to different people and the connections we make with them that break down misconceptions.

Similar to how bias can lead us to do questionable things in our personal lives, bias can wreak the same havoc at work. I've heard the argument that personal biases can somehow be isolated and "locked away" so that they won't cross over into work. Really? How does that work? If I harbor bias against a White guy, how can I say that I will magically check my bias at the door when I'm in the office? If it were so easy, like a switch I can turn on and off, why wouldn't I just check my biases at the door every day? And what if my home *is also* my office? What happens to my biases when I have no safe space to "lock" them away?

While we're on the topic of White guys, I have one more thing to say: yes, we can hold a bias against White males, even if they are considered a majority group. I've done it, and I doubt I'm the only one. I've seen it countless times during diversity training, where White males are hesitant to contribute or are overtly told they have no place in a particular discussion. This is a mistake. When we talk about the importance of diversity, it can't be an "us" versus "them" dichotomy. Embracing diversity isn't a homework assignment strictly for White males. It's a mindset, and it's one we all need to adopt.

Everyone has a diversity story, regardless of whether they are a person who looks like they are or aren't historically marginalized. Not all diversity is above the waterline. For example, a person's sexual orientation, parental status or disability may not be visible to us, but that doesn't make this identity less significant. Diversity and inclusion leader Jennifer Brown captures the sentiment perfectly when talking about diversity:

"We will need everyone. At whatever level, with whatever identity, or in whatever package they're born—everyone is needed to create true culture change... we all want to be welcomed, valued, respected, and heard. And straight, white men, who happen to be the dominant demographic group in American business, are certainly no different."[96]

We all need to observe our environment. If we don't see any diversity, we need to work to change it. Invite people into your life who don't act, think, or look like you. Talk. Empathize. Question. Argue. Listen. Learn.

I'll repeat it. This whole diversity thing isn't just a project solely for majority classes. We all hold the responsibility to stand up for diversity and work toward building compassionate cultures—for the workforce, for ourselves, and for humanity.

---

96 Jennifer Brown, *Inclusion: Diversity, The New Workplace & The Will to Change.* (Hartford: Publish your Purpose Press, 2016), 242-243.

DIVERSITY SETS THE STAGE FOR EQUITABLE WORKFORCES

Growing up, my friends were almost exclusively Indian, partly due to my environment and partly due to my own choosing. I was painfully shy and self-conscious as a kid, and I thought that if I surrounded myself with other people who looked like me, I would be less likely to be judged. (Life lesson: When you have braces, a bad haircut, bad glasses, and a bad wardrobe, no amount of cultural homogeneity will save you.)

I'm an adult now, with three kids of my own. Based on my own experiences and mistakes, I've learned the value of "cross-group" friendships. Elizabeth Page Gould and Rodolfo Mendoza Denton, Ph.D., studied this at length.[97] When discussing the importance of combatting prejudice and embracing diversity, Rodolfo points to the effectiveness of intergroup friendships, based on the premise that contact reduces prejudices.[98]

Hundreds of studies have now shown the powerful effects of intergroup contact.[99] The thinking is that true friendships are built when people get to know one another, share common goals, and cooperate in activities that support and strengthen their bonds. Rodolfo states that the impact of intergroup friendships on prejudice are contagious: if your friend has

---

97 Elizabeth Page-Gould and Rodolfo Mendoza-Denton. "Cross-Race Relationships: An Annotated Bibliography," Elizabeth Page-Gould, last modified February 14, 2009.

98 Gordon W. Allport, *The Nature of Prejudice*, 25th Anniversary ed. (New York: Perseus Books, 1979), 23-24.

99 Rodolfo Mendoza-Denton, "This Holiday, a Toast to Cross-Race Friendship," Psychology Today, November 23, 2010.

a cross-race friend, and you learn about that friendship, your *own* level of prejudice is likely to decrease.

Going a little deeper, when we diversify the people we work with, play with, and connect with, we begin to integrate them into our own self- in other words, we see them as part of our own orbits. This happens naturally as we communicate and get to know others. Their ups and downs are literally our own. We feel their pain. We feel proud of their accomplishments. It's part of a natural process called *self-expansion.*[100]

Diversity matters, but it won't magically appear at work because we issued a statement about it. We need to build it into our DNA, which starts with immersing ourselves and our children in diverse experiences, socializing with people, and integrating new perspectives into our lives. When we do that, building and sustaining a diverse workplace won't feel like a mandate. It will feel right. It will be organic.

When I look at the school calendar our local county hands out every year, I see multiple languages. I see multiple holidays from multiple cultures. On more than one occasion, my kids reminded me about our own upcoming Indian holidays, ones that I may have forgotten without their help. They've also reminded me of notable holidays from other cultures and spoken to me about what foods their friends ate, what they did, and how they celebrated. It's a small gesture, but it's actions like these that expose us to diversity. Given today's younger generation's life experiences, it seems likely that

---

100 "Identity," Psychology Today, accessed July 29, 2020.

tomorrow's adults won't merely accept diversity. They will demand it.[101]

Will our organizations be ready?

DIVERSITY MATTERS BECAUSE IT HELPS THE BOTTOM LINE

Many companies talk about their commitment to diversity, but if you took a look at your organization, at how leadership looks at the top, or at how people are treated, what would you see?

In the summer of 2017, Google Software Engineer James Damore perceived *too much* diversity. In the months prior, he had been growing increasingly upset over the way Google was seeking to increase the number of minority and women employees, which Damore considered reverse discrimination. "It was wrong for Google to be pursuing diversity because men are naturally better with computers," Damore wrote in a ten-page memo. His report went viral, and Google fired him.[102]

Unless we have met James Damore personally, we can't really speak to the type of person he is, but we can say this: good or bad guy, his memo entirely missed the business case for diversity.

---

101 Christie Smith and Stephanie Turner, "The Radical Transformation of Diversity and Inclusion: The Millennial Influence," Billie Jean King Leadership Initiative, 2015.

102 Owen Jones, "Google's Sexist Memo has Provided the Alt-Right With a New Martyr," The Guardian, August 8, 2017.

For the moment, let's set aside the moral grounds for giving people from different backgrounds a fair shot. (We will get there later.) In a naturally diverse and interconnected world, organizations and institutions with higher diversity levels are attracting stronger candidates and achieving better results.

The business case for diversity is well established. Many countless sources of data and research explain the "whys' of diversity. Below is just a sprinkling:

1. In 2019, *The Wall Street Journal* looked at companies in the S&P 500 stock market index and measured 10 metrics, including representation of women, ethnic diversity, age, and whether the company had diversity programs in place. The results? Diverse and inclusive cultures provide companies with a competitive edge over their peers. Specifically, the 20 most diverse companies in the research not only had better-operating results on average than the lowest-scoring firms, but their shares generally outperformed those of the least diverse firms.[103]

2. The millennial and Gen Z generations are the most diverse we've ever had in America: only 56 percent of the 87 million millennials in the country are White, compared to 72 percent of the 76 million members of the baby boomer generation.[104]

3. 67 percent of job seekers state that workplace diversity is important when considering job opportunities, and

---

103 Dieter Holger, "The Business Case for More Diversity," The Wall Street Journal, October 26, 2019.

104 Annalyn Kurtz and Tal Yellin, "Millennial Generation are Bigger, More Diverse than Boomers," CNN Business, accessed July 28, 2020.

more than 50 percent of current employees want their workplace to improve their diversity numbers.[105]

4. Organizations with above-average gender diversity out-perform companies with below-average diversity by 46 percent to 58 percent.[106]

Almost every profession I can think of thrives on innovation. Diversity is the key because when multiple backgrounds and perspectives are represented, you will get a broader range of creative approaches to a problem. Diversity also helps make sound decisions. Not quick and easy decisions, but sound decisions based on a wide range of perspectives and experiences. Diverse teams also create better products and services that reflect the communities they serve. For example, would you want to buy tampons from a company with no women on their product development team? Diversity is more than a metric; it is actually an integral part of a successful revenue-generating business. This makes perfect sense—when you approach a problem from multiple perspectives and angles, you are more likely to find a solution that works.[107]

DIVERSITY MATTERS BECAUSE IT'S THE RIGHT THING TO DO

The word "diversity" can be a very personal and visceral term, but one thing is certain: it applies to all of us.

---

105 Glassdoor Team, "What Job Seekers Really Think About Your Diversity and Inclusion Stats," Glassdoor, November 17, 2014.

106 Gwen Moran, "How These Top Companies Are Getting Inclusion Right," Fast Company, January 23, 2017.

107 Ruthie Miller, Ruthie, "5 Reasons Why Diversity Drives Innovation for Small Businesses," SalesForce, May 2, 2018.

Having a business case is important when talking about the importance of diversity, but let's not forget the strongest reason to embrace diversity: it's the right thing to do.

Every organization wants to be seen as ethical. We try to determine whether our choices are right or wrong, good or bad. Some researchers spend their entire professional lives studying the science of ethical decision-making. They find that ethical decision-making is influenced by both the individual and their environment, and diversity is at its center.

The most informative study I came across was a 2012 study that looked at diversity in ethical decision-making in the workplace. The study went into great detail, describing why we need multiple perspectives when faced with ethical and safety dilemmas. They proposed that group diversity may, in fact, be the key to ethical decision-making in the workplace, specifically because people from different backgrounds bring unique perspectives, experiences, and information when discussing and studying ethical issues that might be lacking in homogenous groups.[108]

Let's get more specific with this line of thought. Diversity can lead to more ethical decision making. In the wake of George Floyd's murder in May of 2020, there was a deeper look into police officers' makeup, and a startling statistic came up: women make up just 12.6 percent of all police officers.[109]

---

108 Sandra Degrassi et al. "Ethical Decision-Making: Group Diversity Holds the Key," *Journal of Leadership, Accountability, and Ethics* 9, no. 6 (2012): 51-65.

109 Rosa Brooks, "One Reason for Police Violence? Too Many Men with Badges," The Washington Post, June 18, 2020.

Professor Rosa Brooks, Co-director of the Georgetown Innovative Policing Program, studied this topic and noted that though officers' racial makeup is certainly important, gender diversity can also have a powerful impact. One finding? Women were often very skilled at navigating high conflict situations, and their communication skills were often extremely well-suited to de-escalating heated moments. A simple way to achieve a less violent and more equitable form of law enforcement could simply include hiring women. Of course, gender isn't destiny, and Rosa reiterated: "Every officer, regardless of gender, can and should be expected to police respectfully and with restraint, and statistics tell us nothing about how a given individual is likely to behave."[110]

The diversity statistics in the US police force and workforce in general tell us that we are all armed with the benefits of diversity. A diversity training workshop, though useful, isn't enough. Workforces need to make explicit commitments to champion diversity because it's safe, it's right, and it's in the best interests of any organization. Explicit commitments include things like publishing your data, so progress can be shared and measured. Publishing this type of data shows a company's transparency and also helps root out diversity-related infrastructure problems (like recruiting candidates primarily from expensive schools and conferences that price many people out).

When diverse perspectives are included, respected, and valued, we get a better grasp of the "big picture," and we better

---

110 Ibid.

understand the people we serve, what they need, and how to successfully meet people where they are.[111]

One example of a leader embracing both diversity and transparency is Janice Bryant Howroyd. Janice is best known for being the first African American woman to self-start a *multi-billion* -dollar business. She is the founder and CEO of The ActOne Group, the largest privately held, minority woman-owned human resource company, which focuses on recruiting talent and technology that employs predictive analytics to support companies' hiring and planning.

Not only does Janice Bryant Howroyd have her finger on the pulse of diversity, but she has also used her focus on diversity when making tough decisions throughout her organization.

I interviewed Janice in 2019. When I asked about diversity, she said that innovation requires a new way of looking at things, and there is no way to think outside the box if everyone thinks, sounds, and acts like you. Diversity and inclusion are the foundations on which her company is built, and she feels a deep sense of responsibility to lead the way so others may follow.

Janice's company seeks out employees with diverse backgrounds and encourages them to bring their unique perspective to their operations. When I asked her about her definition of success, she said, "Success is the progressive realization of worthy ideals." Part of realizing worthy ideals includes "circular, complete communication" in which you

---

111 Brene Brown, *Dare to Lead: Brave Work. Tough Conversations. Whole Hearts.* (New York: Random House, 2018), 13-36.

always talk to people directly and connect with intention. It's open and it's transparent. That's how she runs her multi-billion-dollar empire.

After talking to Janice, I started thinking about all the companies doing the opposite of what Janice was doing and how they had been fraught with corporate scandals (Enron, HP, WorldCom, to name a few). People within those organizations made some bad choices. Maybe they knew what they were doing was wrong, or perhaps some of the issues were morally confusing. I keep thinking, though: would things have been different if there were more diverse voices at the table to sift through choices and consequences? Who's to say. One thing is clear: ethical dilemmas will continue to happen at work. It's in all of our best interests to have more heterogeneity to help guide us to the light, especially as our workforces cross cities, state lines, and country borders.

REMOTE DIVERSITY

Technology is just one industry typically known for embracing remote work. That may have permanently changed with the coronavirus, as remote work has become common for millions of people, seemingly overnight.

Distributed/remote work is a force we will all likely experience. Twitter CEO Jack Dorsey sent an email to the company's 4,900 employees in May of 2020, saying many of them would be allowed to work from home permanently.[112]

---

112   Rae Hodge, Rae, "Twitter Makes Work from Home a Permanent Change for Some Employees," CNET, May 12, 2020.

Dorsey said: "We were uniquely positioned to respond quickly and allow folks to work from home given our emphasis on decentralization and supporting a distributed workforce capable of working from anywhere. The past few months have proven we can make that work."

Twitter is hardly alone. Companies like Facebook, Slack, Square, and Google have followed suit by allowing some, or most, employees to work remotely.[113]

Diversity in remote work matters. Going remote allows organizations to better embrace variances in gender, race, ethnicity, sexual identity, and ability. It provides improved creativity, a more comprehensive range of skills, increased employee engagement, improved company reputation, and even financial benefits.

The problem right now is that companies like the idea of diversity, but they're trying to fit diversity into a pre-existing structure. The basic principles of diversity do apply, but to implement diversity in a remote workforce, we need to also consider the following:

In a distributed/remote workforce, location becomes a new element of diversity. If you are a tech company that employs people living in Silicon Valley, and you are now hiring nationally or internationally, you will get a diverse group of people and perspectives. Distributed work opens the door for anyone who fits your hiring criteria: This could be a rural worker, a foreign worker, or a working parent.

---

113 Ibid.

This could be a worker with physical or sensory disabilities who can now take over a wide range of roles while allowing others' neurodiversity to bring another layer of diversity to a company's culture. People with disabilities represent an untapped and robust talent pool, which can add substantial value to an organization. We have the chance to seize on that opportunity.

Diversity is also essential in remote/distributed workforces because it offers us a chance to toss the outdated "who knows who" approach that often happens with local, new, and lateral hiring. Forty-five percent of American workers experienced discrimination and harassment in the past year of their employment.[114] Tossing the "who knows who" roadmap allows a broader range of voices to be heard, hired, and promoted.

Whether you're working remotely, in an office, or a combination of the two, diversity matters. As a society, we've made some real progress, but we still have a lot of work to do to take full advantage of the opportunity that a more diverse workforce represents. We live in a deeply connected and global world. It should come as no surprise that more diverse companies and institutions are achieving better performance.

The time to invest in diversity is right now—those who don't take this opportunity risk becoming irrelevant or non-existent in the future.

---

114 "Build a Culture Where Every Employee Can Use Their Voice," Gallup, accessed July 29, 2020.

CHAPTER SIX

WHY DOES INCLUSION MATTER?

———

"Inclusivity means not just 'we're allowed to be there,' but we are valued. I've always said: smart teams will do amazing things, but truly diverse teams will do impossible things."

—RYAN HADFIELD[115]

My family always makes fun of me because it takes me all day to drink a cup of coffee. I generally grab my coffee around sunrise and am somehow usually still nursing the same cup hours later when the sun sets.

It's not really about the caffeine for me. I find the smell of coffee and the feel of the cup really comforting.

Usually.

———

115 Ryan Hadfield, "45 Quotes from LGBTQ+ Leaders About Diversity and Inclusion in Business." Zoominfo. October 10, 2019.

In 2019, my kids and I were about halfway through our drive from Cleveland back to DC. Despite the rain, we needed to get out of the car to stretch, so I pulled over at a nearby rest stop. We went to a well-known coffee shop so I could get some coffee. I ordered a cappuccino, and then the barista asked me for my name.

"It's Anjali," I said. "It's spelled A-N-J-A-L-I."

"Woah, what?" she said.

"An-ja-li. It sounds like Un-jelly," I told her as I spelled my name again.

"Oh girl, I'm not even gonna try to say or spell that!" the barista laughed.

I was dumbstruck. "Well technically, you don't have to try since I literally just said my name, repeated it and spelled it so...."

She cut me off. "Well, you're lucky your drink isn't complicated, or I would have just refused to help you!" she chuckled.

I looked outside. It was still pouring. At that moment, I looked at my kids and decided it wasn't worth prolonging the torturous interaction. I just wanted to get the heck out of there and get home. As I walked over to the pick-up counter to grab my drink, I saw the name "A-Julie" scrawled across the side of the cup. I winced, looked at my kids, and decided I didn't want a public confrontation in my kids' presence. They didn't seem to notice my reaction because they continued their normal behavior, rushing toward the exit, racing to see who would be first to press the silver and blue push plate that automatically opened the door.

As we crossed into the DC area several hours later, my normally comforting coffee cup seemed to be taunting me, like it was trying to ask: "Hey A-JULIE, what's good, girl?" I couldn't even bear to look at it anymore.

My emotions toward that coffee shop incident have nothing to do with the barista not spelling or pronouncing my name. Name issues happen regularly, and it's almost always without malice or ill will. It's honestly no big deal most of the time.

This particular interaction was different because of the barista's dismissive tone. She made it seem like it was *my* fault that I had the audacity to have an unfamiliar name, and the problem wasn't her inability to say my name; it was *me*.

Conscious or not, name biases often exist. I have grown resigned to it: I think of it as a name tax, pay it and move on. But the reality is that my name isn't Julie, and one day after 100 people have said my name wrong, someone is going to call me Julie or Angela, and I'm going to react, and it will probably seem out of line. When this happens, I may tell you that it feels like death by a million cuts when people don't bother to ask you how to say your real name, or worse—they ask and then don't care. Maybe I'll say all of that to you, but maybe I won't have it in me, and I'll leave you with no explanation at all.

Mispronouncing a name may sound like a little thing. But as Nike and Stephen Curry will tell you, little things have a funny way of adding up. In 2013, NBA superstar Stephen Curry left an extremely lucrative deal with Nike to join Under Armour. Why? Apparently, one of the reasons was because a Nike official didn't take the time to learn to pronounce Curry's first name at a pitch meeting, calling him "Steph-on" when his name is pronounced "Steffen."[116]

"Little things" like names are important. As communities and societies become more globalized, the likelihood that we will meet someone whose name we can't pronounce will increase. There is a reasonable expectation that we won't try to change someone's name to make life more convenient for *us*.

Going back to the coffee shop episode, I'm reminded of the contrast I see at my local cafe. There's a guy named Brandon who works there. When I first met Brandon, he didn't try to change my name to suit his own preferences. He just asked me to spell it and listened when I replied.

Whenever he sees me, he always looks me in the eyes and says, "Good to see you, Anjali." And he pronounces my name perfectly every time.

From our very first encounter, Brandon took the time to listen, connect, and care. Those little acts of appreciation Brandon displayed? Kind of a big deal.

---

116 Nate Scott, "The Story of how Nike Lost Stephen Curry is Unbelievable," For the Win, March 23, 2016.

INCLUSION MATTERS BECAUSE EVERYONE HAS THE RIGHT TO FEEL CONNECTED

Inclusion is about accepting and celebrating people's complex selves. At work, it includes the act of hiring and trying to put in fair practices at work. Inclusion is our attempt to welcome and acknowledge what makes us diverse and makes the workplace welcoming and fair. So, inclusion is where we think about evolving our culture through different perspectives, instead of having those different perspectives conform to our existing systems.

In the chapter about the crossroads of diversity and inclusion, I talked about how as a young associate, I attended a professional development organization's Diversity Day but seemed to be the only one who got the memo to dress accordingly. I do believe the event organizers and attendees had good intentions. The problem wasn't with the formulation of these ideas but with the execution.

For me, that particular experience of being the only woman in the group, the only one who threw herself into Diversity Day, was one that I wished I could erase. After Diversity Day, I vowed to be as homogeneous as possible. My goal was to *blend* in to *fit* in.

After Diversity Day, I worked overtime to cover my true self. To blend in, I sometimes pretended to be things I wasn't.

I pretended to like the Chicago Bulls when I was really a Cleveland Cavaliers fan. I pretended to like whiskey even though I prefer wine. I pretended to enjoy car restorations even though I can't even change a flat tire. Why did I do so much pretending? Part of the reason was baseline insecurity with myself, but the bigger part was because people were networking with clients through these channels, and I didn't want to miss out. Eventually, one thing piled on top of another until the person I was at work and at networking events had almost nothing in common with the person I was at home.

This feeling that you are unable to bring your authentic self to work wears on you. It impacts your ability to connect with others. It impacts your productivity. It impacts your longevity with your employer. It's exhausting.

Kenji Yoshino studied this exact issue of masking in the workforce and found that 61 percent of employees in the United States were found to cover some aspect of their authentic selves and who they are while at work. When employees downplay their authentic selves, they negatively impact a workplace's overall productivity, innovation, and ability to build strong and meaningful relationships with colleagues.[117] More than a few years have passed since I was that young associate. I'm now a mom of three kids. I've stopped hiding that part of my life at work, and I've stopped seeing motherhood as a professional liability. I bring up my identity as a mom a lot more than I used to, and I don't hesitate to give colleagues my cell phone number, which has a voicemail of my kids singing, "Mommy's not here! Mommy's not here!" It's been cathartic to slowly embrace my whole self at work. Watching others do the same has been empowering.

---

117   Christie Smith and Kenji Yoshino, "Uncovering Talent: A New Model of Inclusion," Deloitte, 2019.

Employers need to start asking, "Who are you, and how can you embrace your differentiators to excel?" Because if they don't, they may lose some of the most valuable people in their workforce.

WITHOUT INCLUSION, YOU WILL LOSE YOUR MOST VALUABLE ASSETS: YOUR PEOPLE

No matter who you are, you are multidimensional. No one is just one thing. Each of us belongs to several different identity groups. We are all multi-hyphenated and have multiple identities like race, gender, age, and political stances. Depending on our environment, our multi-hyphenated selves have a leg up in some situations, while being oppressed in others, with some being on the short end of the stick far more often. More often than not, our intersecting identities sometimes allow us to experience privilege, while at other times, they put us at an unfair disadvantage.[118]

Let's look at 2020 and the impact of Black Lives Matter on the workforce and humanity. When we see Black people being mistreated and abused and do nothing about it, social turmoil will follow. The results for workplaces who ignore our need for a humane approach to work simply won't survive.

Companies have responded. Entire industries have done the same. For all the companies who have taken public stands against violence and systemic racism, have their actions been consistent with their words? How many of these companies

---

118 Perry Rhodes, Belonging at Work: Everyday Actions You Can Take to Cultivate an Inclusive Organization, (Portland: RPC Academy Press, 2018).

have addressed tangible and correctable issues, like the minority pay gap?[119]

How many companies have diversified their leadership teams? As of 2020, Facebook had one Black person operating in a C-suite level capacity, which refers to a company's most important senior executives. Google had one Black person performing at a C-suite level capacity. Amazon? Zero Black people in C-suite. The same for Microsoft: zero.[120]

Inclusion matters because it's a critical piece of building a compassionate culture, and without it, we will lose the people we need most in the workforce. Simply speaking, the talk won't be enough. Not anymore.

INCLUSION MATTERS BECAUSE DISCONNECTED AND EXCLUDED PEOPLE WON'T STAY

Racial minorities aren't the only ones who feel the sting of exclusion. Early in 2020, I was on a private Facebook group for women lawyers with kids. The topic? The constant feeling of being overwhelmed and the lack of empathy for our multidimensional lives.

Women felt that they could never get enough done at work and never be present enough at home. The comments were coming in so fast and furious that I could barely keep up:

---

119 Ashleigh Webber, Ashleigh, "Ethnicity Pay Gap Reporting: Firms Urged Not to Wait for Legislation," Personnel Today, February 26, 2020.

120 Phil Wahba, "The number of Black CEOs in the Fortune 500 Remains Very Low," Fortune, June 1, 2020.

"The fact that I feel like I'm bending over backward for my entire family, and it's just not enough. My 4 y/o lived her BEST LIFE when I was home on maternity leave with her little sister this summer and is now constantly yelling at me or crying that she misses me when I'm at work. And working full time with two children is way harder than one. I'm hanging on by a thread..."[121]

Another mom said:

"Where to begin... 3 kids 9, 7, 5. I'm the 75 percent parent with all the driving, scheduling, etc. I work a full-time civil litigation job and am hanging on by a very thin thread pretty much daily."[122]

Many of these lawyer moms are in Big Law, not as partners, but as associates.[123] Why haven't many of these moms made partner? Well, there could be a lot of reasons, so let's avoid speculating. Instead, let's look at some cold, hard numbers: According to Law360's "2017 Glass Ceiling Report," women's share of equity partnerships—where the highest compensation and leadership positions are lodged—is still at 20 percent and has not changed in recent years even though over 50 percent of law school graduates are women.[124]

Sadly, big law firms' inability to reach their desired goals of increasing the number of women is not surprising. When the

---

121 Fishbowl Media, LLC. "Fishbowl." Fishbowlapp.com, Vers. 6.2.0 (2016).
122 Ibid.
123 Ibid.
124 "Women See Another Year of Slow Gains At Law Firms," Law 360, July 23, 2017.

diversity rankings are released each year, Big Law reminds us that White men still dominate today's biggest firms, and firms' efforts to change haven't been substantial enough.

Big Law mottos often go something like this: Anybody can be the next big partner, just as long as you pull the long billable hours, and procure the most business, which often means endless late nights at various dinners and events.

But what if you have 3 kids and an aging parent to take care of, and you can't burn the midnight oil at the office every night of the week? Hmm, well, things might get trickier for you if you fall into that camp, like this mom:

"I just always feel like I'm just barely on top of it at work. Before having kids, I always felt way ahead of the game, but now... I'm just barely keeping my head above water. I can't have that face time at work at 9 pm each night, and even though I'm at home working, it's still not enough. I am missing out on networking opportunities that could help my career."[125]

Lawyers are not in a league of their own. The issue of gender imbalance affects every industry across every area. Although some companies are making encouraging improvements to their culture, we still haven't seen enough companies offer concrete solutions to the problem (like increased flex time, mid-day wellness breaks, nixing mandatory meetings past 5 pm, valuing efficiency over billable hours, etc.)

---

125 Fishbowl Media, LLC. "Fishbowl." Fishbowlapp.com, Vers. 6.2.0 (2016).

Some of each industry's best women are leaving their professions because the proverbial thread they are barely hanging onto is slipping from their grip. They feel like they have no one to talk to, and no one who cares.

In fact, Gallup's 2017 "State of the American Workplace" report revealed that just 4 in 10 employees believe that their supervisor or someone at work seems to care about them as a person.[126] This may be, in part, because many workplace cultures often overtly or implicitly discourage friendship, especially across hierarchical lines. So do certain professions. One 2018 survey of 1,624 full-time employees found that the loneliest workers by far were those with degrees in law and medicine.[127]

Apart from the emotional toll exclusion takes on individuals, it's also bad for business. A 2018 Wharton study by Dr. Sigal Barsade shows that excluded employees feel less committed to their work and coworkers. When social ties begin to fray among colleagues, distrust infects communications and collaboration. Entire teams and even departments can suffer.[128]

Gallup's report, "Why We Need Best Friends at Work," found that having positive personal relationships was among the most important factors in employee engagement, alongside personal development opportunities and inclusion.

---

126 "State of the American Workplace," Gallup, 2017.
127 Even W. Carr et al., "The Value of Belonging at Work," Harvard Business Review, December 16, 2019.
128 Hakan Ozcelik and Sigal G. Barsade, "No Employee an Island: Workplace Loneliness and Job Performance," *Academy of Management Journal* 61, no. 6 (December 2018).

Gallup further found that when workers are respected, and the culture values the relationship, friendships can generate innovative discussions that benefit the team and the organization and individuals. In other words, workers' social health is closely intertwined with inclusion and the workplace's overall health.[129]

Having a sense of inclusion and belonging is not a soft "nice to have." As humans, it's a basic need to belong. Not just for working moms. Not just for racial minorities. Not just for disabled employees. Not just for a White man struggling with wellbeing. Belonging is necessary for all of us. Will we find empathy and compassion for other's multi-dimensionality? Are we willing to pay the price if we don't?

INCLUSION/BELONGING MATTERS BECAUSE WE NEED CONNECTION IN A DISTRIBUTED WORKFORCE

If we struggle to connect and communicate in person, how will we handle tomorrow's largely remote workforce? Over the past 20 years, collaborative activities now account for 75 percent of an employer's day-to-day work, but more and more of that is happening over apps and social media, not in person.[130]

Remote work can bring substantial benefits to an organization by allowing it to look beyond its headquarters to attract top talent. Still, remote workers also face unique challenges

---

129 Annamarie Mann, "Why We Need Best Friends at Work," Gallup, January 15, 2018.

130 Rob Cross et al., "Collaborative Overload," Harvard Business Review, January 2016.

and feel isolated and disconnected from their companies. Inclusion for remote workers matters because it's a key to retaining them.[131] While leading an all-remote company will require many managers to rethink and rework how they run their businesses, all-remote is possible and can lead to greater resilience to crises and an increased sense of connection to others and the company itself.

So much talent resides outside of major metropolitan areas, and this pool will suddenly be able to compete for high-paying and rewarding jobs at the world's leading companies. This talent will get the chance to connect with people from different demographics and cultures, all while staying anchored to the local communities they love.[132]

Technology has lulled us into a false sense of comfort that we are all highly connected, but in reality, many feel isolated from our colleagues. What people crave most, and what research increasingly shows to be the key to successful workplace cultures, is a sense of authentic connection with others.

In the age of globalization, being aware of and acknowledging others' cultural differences is more important than ever. This is especially true for leaders, whose job is to understand and manage nuances within their teams.[133] Inclusion and belonging matter for remote workers because, despite the

131 Joseph Grenny and David Maxfield, "A Study of 1,000 Employees Found That Remote Workers Feel Shunned and Left Out," Harvard Business Review, November 2, 2017.
132 Sid Sijbrandij, "Hybrid Remote Work Offers the Worst of Both Worlds," Wired, July 12, 2020.
133 Erin Meyer, The Culture Map: Breaking Through the Invisible Boundaries of Global Business. (Philadelphia: Perseus Books, 2014).

naysayers' belief that feelings don't belong in the workplace (remote or in-person), science says otherwise.[134]

We have direct neurological connections between our feelings, thoughts, and actions. Frustration, alienation through being "othered," and stress make us shut down. When this happens, we just don't think as clearly or engage as well.[135]

Leaders, managers, and employees all have the responsibility to ensure that remote employees are being included in the conversations, projects, and big shifts.[136] There's a saying that goes something like, "Employees join a company, but they leave a boss." Here's the thing about walking away from a relationship, whether it's with a person or an organization: making that decision to end things can be hard. But once the decision is made? You are unlikely to get that person back.

After all, there's no way to hang onto someone who is no longer yours to hold.

134 Daniel Goleman, *Destructive Emotions: A Scientific Dialogue with the Dalai Lama* (New York: Bantam Books, 2003).

135 Daniel Goleman et al., *Primal Leadership, With a New Preface by the Authors: Unleashing the Power of Emotional Intelligence* (Boston: Harvard Business Review, 2013).

136 "How Managers Trump Companies," Gallup, August 12, 1999.

CHAPTER SEVEN

WHY DOES WELLBEING MATTER?

"Wellness is the cake, not the icing."

- DR. LARRY RICHARD[137]

Gabriel MacConaill ("Gabe") was a husband, friend, and partner at the law firm Sidley Austin. He shot himself in the head in October of 2018.

Before his death, Gabe had been working on a complicated case. He wasn't sleeping as much, he was isolating himself, and he felt like he was breaking down. Perfectionism is a common trait in the legal profession and many others. Although Gabe was a respected bankruptcy partner at a large law firm, Gabe's wife recalled how he felt like a phony who would never reach those perfect ideals. He was scared that if he appeared weak, he might lose his job. Gabe's wife was

---

137 "Resources." Lawyer Brain. Accessed September 5, 2020.

worried about him and had actually suggested that he quit his job, but he said he couldn't quit in the middle of a case. "The irony is not lost on me that he found it easier to kill himself..." his wife stated.

In an open letter to the profession, Gabe's widowed wife Joanna stated simply and conclusively: "Big Law killed my husband."[138] The impact of his death extended way past his family. After his death, other Sidley employees in the LA office also quit, saying:

"The firm's leadership did not respond sufficiently in the wake of his (Gabriel's) death, and there was no clear commitment to support employees who... found the (firm's) corporate culture an unwelcome environment in which to 'raise a hand' to seek help."[139]

There's a little bit of Gabe in all of us. Joanna remembers her husband as someone who lived his life with integrity and treated people with compassion, kindness, and authenticity. She believes her husband died feeling overworked and undervalued.[140]

Gabe was hardly alone in how he felt. Fields like law, medicine, banking, and countless others are prone to intense levels of stress. Jeffrey Pfeffer, a professor at Stanford University,

---

138 Joanna Litt, Joanna, "'Big Law Killed My Husband': An Open Letter From a Sidley Partner's Widow," Law.com, November 12, 2018.

139 Lilah Raptopoulos and James Fontanella-Khan, "The Trillion-Dollar Taboo: Why it's Time to Stop Ignoring Mental Health at Work," Financial Times, July 10, 2019.

140 Joanna Litt, Joanna, "'Big Law Killed My Husband': An Open Letter From a Sidley Partner's Widow," Law.com, November 12, 2018.

doesn't mince words. He unapologetically states: "The workplace is the single biggest source of stress in America."[141]

Employers, too often, aren't aware or aren't doing enough to help. Studies show that 1 in 4 adults experience mental illness throughout their lives.[142] And unfortunately, most people aren't open about their issues with anxiety, depression, and stress, and do their best to hide any problems that come up while they're on the clock. When dealing with mental health challenges, there seems to be a growing sense of the "don't ask, don't tell" mindset that leads to conditions like depression and disabling anxiety to get swept under the rug.

Some companies do have wellbeing resources in place, but without a compassionate culture of caring and empathy, people may not feel comfortable enough to take advantage of available help. In other words, help may be available, but it will be hard to get people to reach for it if it doesn't seem easily accessible. Too many people stay quiet when they need to talk. They suffer alone when they need to be heard.

Taking care of our wellbeing, especially our mental health, can be a serious challenge for companies and employees. So, whether or not you've noticed these problems at your place of business, it's pretty safe to bet that wellbeing affects your workplace, especially given the 2020 global pandemic and ensuing economic recession.

---

141 Jeffrey Pfeffer, *Dying for a Paycheck: How Modern Management Harms Employee Health and Company Performance—and What We Can Do About It* (New York: HarperCollins, 2018), 33-36.
142 "Mental Health Disorder Statistics," Johns Hopkins Medicine, accessed August 2, 2020.

Some industries are beginning to listen and to take action. In 2019, New Jersey Attorney General Gurbir Grewal created a proactive statewide program designed to bolster law enforcement officers' resiliency to mental health issues, saying "protecting an officer's mental health is just as important as guarding their physical safety."[143]

The NBA also responded by bolstering its mental health services after players like Kevin Love and DeMar DeRozan spoke up about their own mental health struggles. The NBA now requires teams to have licensed mental health workers for players.

"Sometimes... it gets the best of you, where there's times everything in the whole world's on top of you. It's one of (those) things that no matter how indestructible we look like we are, we're all human at the end of the day," Toronto Raptors All-Star DeMar DeRozan reported.[144]

Haven't we all felt similarly at some point in our lives, like we are overwhelmed by our inadequacy? Haven't we all felt alone at work before? The stigma associated with mental health challenges often leads people to ignore, dismiss, or under-report their symptoms. People stay quiet when they need to talk. They feel alone when they need to be heard. That is why employers have to take workplace wellbeing seriously. Wellbeing cannot be an afterthought. We have to address it head-on.

---

143 Lilo H. Stainton, "NJ Launches Nation's First Stress 'Resiliency' Program for Police Officers." NJ Spotlight. August 7, 2019.

144 "DeMar DeRozan on inspiring Kevin Love: 'Made Me Feel Pretty Damn Good.'" ESPN. March 7, 2018.

WELLBEING MATTERS BECAUSE OUR PEOPLE MATTER

As Editor-at-Large for Arianna Huffington's *Overcoming Lawyer Burnout* platform, I got to meet a lot of interesting people, many of them experts in their fields. A couple of experts really moved me with their passion and expansive knowledge, and one of those people was Dr. Larry Richard, an expert on the psychology of lawyer behavior. Though his work focuses on attorneys, many of his findings and insights are broadly applicable to anyone looking to improve their individual or collective wellbeing.

When I first met Larry, I expected to see a super formal guy wearing a suit and tie. When we met, though, Larry was dressed casually. His demeanor was light and airy as if he was an old friend from college whom I had already met a hundred times. I realized that the stack of research I was carrying probably wasn't necessary and that what I thought would be an official "note-taking" meeting turned out to be one of the most enlightening and enjoyable conversations I've ever had about wellbeing. We talked about why wellbeing matters, and how it consists of more than adding a massage chair or a bowl of apples to the office kitchen. It's not something you address if and when you have the time, resources, or budget. Wellbeing is a fundamental need for any person at any workplace, every day of every year.

"Wellness is the cake, not the icing," Larry said. In other words, organizations need to put the same focus on wellbeing that they put on profit margins and churn rates. Another thing? Wellbeing isn't about waiting for someone to fall ill or have a breakdown so you can point them to a list of approved medical providers. It's not merely about knowing how to patch up something (or someone) who's broken. The real story is about designing and cultivating a workplace that supports fulfilling and thriving lives to prevent people from breaking down in the first place.

Larry continued to explain that what we need is a "preventative medicine" approach to wellbeing. The practices, policies, and actions that lead to optimal wellbeing also happen to be drivers of profitability, engagement, and retention.

In his article, "Wellness is the Cake, Not the Icing," Larry states that organizations should think about wellbeing as a set of integrated and systematic practices that should be deeply embedded in a firm's culture. Wellbeing should be part of every aspect of a business. "Think of it as the last remaining source of competitive advantage," Larry says.[145]

Humanity through wellbeing as a competitive advantage? Seems morally sound, financially wise, and physically imperative today more than ever.

WELLBEING IMPROVES PRODUCTIVITY

Openness pays. When companies don't encourage open conversations about wellbeing, particularly mental health, they will end up paying in lost profits and productivity. A few facts to consider:

1. A failure to support employees is costing us big time: over 615 million people suffer from depression and anxiety.

145] "Resources." Lawyer Brain. Accessed September 5, 2020.

According to a recent World Health Organization study, this costs an estimated $1 trillion in lost productivity every year.[146]

2. According to the American Psychological Association, companies that do not have systems in place to support their employees' wellbeing have higher turnover, lower productivity, and higher healthcare costs.[147]

3. Evidence shows that investing in employee wellbeing can deliver bottom-line returns. And when companies approach wellbeing as a *core business strategy*, and not solely to lower employer healthcare costs, it can lead to measurable returns on investment (ROI) through higher engagement, lower turnover, and better productivity.[148]

Science backs up the theory that high levels of wellbeing lead to higher productivity, to the tune of gaining almost a day's worth of work each week, according to research by the Advanced Wellbeing Research Center. The study noted that employee energy levels are a barrier to productivity, with a fifth of employees reporting they are tired most of the time. Using the insight of marginal gains, which focuses on incremental improvements to wellbeing, you can see that energy levels and productivity all shot up.[149]

---

146 "Mental Health in the Workplace," World Health Organization, May 2019.

147 American Psychological Association, "Psychologically healthy Workplaces Have Lower Turnover, Less Stress, and Higher Satisfaction," 2011.

148 Tom Rath and Jim Harter, "Wellbeing: The Five Essential Elements," Gallup, accessed August 3, 2020.

149 Simon Alim, "Workplace Wellbeing Can Boost Productivity." FT Adviser, November 23, 2017.

Leaders like Bill Gates or Virgin Pulse's Richard Branson advocate for wellbeing. Companies are learning that the healthier your employees are, the more productive they become.[150]

WELLBEING IMPROVES RECRUITMENT AND RETENTION

People are the most important asset in every organization. When an employer prioritizes the wellbeing of its team, it's like telling people, "We think you're important. We care about your health, your happiness, and your role in this organization."

In recent years, there's been an increasing level of employee interest in wellbeing programs. The argument in favor of wellbeing programs looks like this: businesses benefit from reduced health-related costs from the implementation of wellness programs, and these programs also help with recruiting, engaging, and retaining employees. Companies that help their employees address and oversee various health conditions can earn trust from employees, which will make them work harder, perform better, and miss less work.[151]

Successful organizations are built by ensuring that employees are engaged, healthy, and exposed to a strong workplace culture. The following statistics reiterate why engagement and wellness strategy need to be priorities for your organization:

---

150 Emma Seppälä and Kim Cameron, "Proof That Positive Work Cultures are More Productive," Harvard Business Review, December 1, 2015.

151 "Nearly Half of American Workers See Wellness Programs as an Important Employee Retention Tool," Business Wire, January 14, 2010.

1. Wellbeing programs are one way to address employee wellbeing. Forty-five percent of Americans working at small to medium-sized companies say that they would stay at their jobs longer if there were good employer-sponsored wellness programs.[152]

2. People with higher wellbeing are better workers. People with higher levels of wellbeing become more engaged with their jobs and work harder.[153] In contrast, disgruntled, unhappy workers aren't pleasant to be around, and no one wants to be around others who are constantly spewing negativity.

3. Employees who feel their voices are heard are 4.6 times more likely to feel empowered to perform their best work. Inviting more people to have a seat at a table and listening to what they have to report about their wellbeing, can make them feel that their voices are heard and increase their engagement and connection to their work.[154]

After reading all these stats, you may be convinced that nearly every person at every organization is sold on wellbeing programs, but this wouldn't be entirely accurate. A countermovement to the wellbeing program phenomenon exists, and it's an interesting take. The argument against wellbeing programs looks like this: Too many wellbeing programs are trying to change the worker, instead of changing the work.

152 Stephen Miller, Wellness Programs as an Employee Retention Tool," SHRM, January 20, 2010.

153 Annie Mckee, Annie, "Being Happy at Work Matters," Harvard Business Review, November 14, 2014.

154 Adam Kirsh, "Why Equality and Diversity Need to be SMB Priorities, "Salesforce, February 2, 2018.

Case in point? In 2018, many West Virginia teachers protested, holding up signs that said the following:

"I'd take a BULLET for your child, but PEIA wouldn't cover it!"[155]

The frustration behind the signs came from the fact that many West Virginia teachers felt their jobs were insanely exhausting and stressful, and that the Public Employees Insurance Agency, handling their wellbeing issues, put the onus on *them* to take care of their ensuing issues, making the solution worse than the problem.

A couple of years ago, I read about a guy who used a blowtorch to clear spider webs out of his backyard. He did this successfully, but accidentally set his entire house on fire at the same time. Not a perfect analogy, but this is the same train of thought. Too often, we rush to address the symptom without ever addressing the problem (the real cause of spiders was coming from the fact that the homeowner turned on too many outdoor lights at night, which attracted insects, making the free food source irresistible for the spiders. He could have just turned off the countless outdoor lights instead of burning his house down).[156]

Whatever your stance on wellbeing programs may be, one thing should be clear to all of us: wellbeing itself always matters. Studies by the US Centers for Disease Control and

155 Olivia Kan-Sperling, "Sick Days: Individualized Healthcare and Corporatized Well-Being," The College Hill Independent, March 15, 2018.
156 Eric Pfeiffer, "Man Sets House on Fire After Using Blowtorch on Spider Webs," Yahoo! News, July 10, 2012.

Prevention and others demonstrate that wellbeing—a combination of physical, mental, and spiritual health—is of primary importance in the workplace.[157]

Think about how a workforce with high levels of wellbeing looks to the next wave of employees at your company: it's a recruitment message that screams, "People like being here!" No amount of Facebook advertisements can convey that as well as the employees. Glassdoor and similar sites are aggregating employee survey data on companies. If you take care of your employees, people will know it. If you don't, people will hear about it. What employees say about a company directly influences who you attract and who you lose.

REMOTE WELLBEING MATTERS

The increase in remote and distributed work resulting from the COVID-19 pandemic that struck the world in 2020 also brought a parallel increase in wellbeing concerns. Stress levels related to childcare, school, safety, and caring for elderly relatives skyrocketed. Women were hit particularly hard by these pandemic concerns. In response, many companies adopted long-term remote work policies: Google, Facebook, and Twitter are just a few tech giants to make the announcement.[158]

The workplace isn't what (or where) it used to be and, post-coronavirus, it likely never will be again. Workers, even

---

157 "Wellbeing Concepts," Centers for Disease Control and Prevention, accessed August 3, 2020.

158 Anneken Tappe, "The Coronavirus Recession is Hitting Women the Hardest." CNN Business. May 11, 2020.

remote ones, still need to feel like they are part of a community.

A recent Gallup poll found that 43 percent of employees work remotely at least some of the time, a trend that is increasing across industries. For many people, especially younger workers, flexible scheduling and remote opportunities aren't just sought-after; they're a must.[159]

For remote workers, some of the most important drivers of worker wellbeing are belonging, appreciation, and inclusion, which are all fundamentally social. Together, these factors help workers feel more confident about their future with a company and reduce isolation and speculation during uncertain times.

Technology has created an illusion that today's employees are highly connected and, maybe in some superficial ways, we are… but the reality is that we don't engage with one another more deeply nearly as much as we need to. We spend a lot of time feeling isolated and alienated.

Wellbeing for remote workers matters because workplace loneliness is spreading. One study by Remote.com showed that 70 percent of remote employees felt left out of the workplace because communication with colleagues was weak. They were being excluded from meetings because of their location.[160] The result was an isolation epidemic that reduced

159 Adam Hickman, "Is Working Remotely Effective? Gallup Research Says Yes," Gallup, January 24, 2020.
160 Tanya Connor, "Loneliness: A New Challenge for the Remote Workplace." Remote How. June 2019.

the percentage of people who said they had a close friend and left half of all Americans feeling lonely.

Dr. Vivek Murthy, former Surgeon General of the United States, says, "Loneliness and weak social connections are associated with a reduction in lifespan, similar to that caused by smoking 15 cigarettes a day."[161]

Think about that. And that's not all. Loneliness not only impacts our mental health, but it can also impact our physical health.

Leaders with newly remote workforces can't just pour money into gym memberships, napping pods, or standing desks to improve wellbeing. They have to ask: what are their people really craving?

What we crave most, what research increasingly shows to be the biggest asset to the workplace culture and wellbeing, is a sense of authentic connection to others.

Employees are over 20 percent more productive when they are happier and connected—and this is also true for remote workers.[162] It's not that we should walk away from technology—in a remote world, we really can't—it's that we can learn how to use it appropriately so we can build connections and empathy so that we can use technology as our servant and not our master.

---

161 Vivek H. Murthy, Vivek H. *Together: The Healing Power of Human Connection in a Sometimes Lonely World* (New York: Harper Wave, 2020).

162 Jan Emmanuel De Neve, "Why Wellbeing Matters and How to Improve It," Said Business School, March 6, 2020.

Here's the wrap up on the data, statistics, and stories: wellbeing matters for everyone in the workforce. To retain the best talent, people have to know that their whole lives are valued and that they can confidently bring their whole selves to work.

An enormous amount of research supports the benefits of wellbeing. A comprehensive focus on wellbeing improves employee health and morale and improves an organization's bottom line. Data is important to any business, but it's important to note that wellbeing is not like cashing a check: you may not see the metrics right away.

In my work consulting clients on wellbeing issues, I'm often asked how to address their desire for data-driven results. When it comes to wellbeing, data is a bit of a lagging indicator. We can measure blood pressure and glucose levels all day long, but those numbers won't give us the low down on how someone is actually doing. It doesn't tell us about a person's struggles, challenges, or successes.

Although it's important to address the business case for wellbeing, it's worth asking: do we really need a "business case" for treating people well? Shouldn't we help our employees simply because it's the right thing to do? Employees are going to start interviewing their employers the same way employers interview them, and they will start saying: "If you really care about our wellbeing, don't just help us deal with our problems. Help us prevent and solve them."

As time goes on, more employees are demanding that their companies do better and be better, even outside of business hours. That's going to require companies to be more than socially responsible. It's going to require them to be compassionate. It's going to require them to be human.

PART THREE

THE "HOWS" OF DIVERSITY, INCLUSION, AND WELLBEING

CHAPTER EIGHT

HOW TO IMPROVE DIVERSITY

———

"Unity, not uniformity, must be our aim. We attain unity only through variety. Differences must be integrated, not annihilated, not absorbed.

- MARY PARKER FOLLETT[163]

On February 20, 2018, *Sports Illustrated* released a bombshell article chronicling almost two decades of workplace misconduct and sexual harassment within the Dallas Mavericks basketball organization. The article called the working atmosphere at the Mavericks organization "disturbing and heartbreaking."[164]

---

163 Darshana Dutta, "25 Powerful Diversity and Inclusion Quotes for a Stronger Company Culture." Vantage Circle. Last modified June 18, 2020.

164 Jon Wertheim and Jessica Luther, "Exclusive: Inside the Corrosive Workplace Culture of the Dallas Mavericks," Sports Illustrated, February 20, 2018.

Several days after the article was published, the Mavericks retained two law firms, Krutoy Law P.C. and Lowenstein Sandler, to conduct an independent investigation into the article's allegations and any other allegations of serious workplace misconduct they may uncover.[165]

The firms spent over seven months interviewing over 200 witnesses, including current and former Mavericks employees, and several other people claiming to have the relevant knowledge to assist in the investigation. They also reviewed over 1.6 million documents, human resource files, handbooks, employee data on hiring and firing, promotions, bonuses, and salary increases.

Throughout the investigation, the law firms maintained steady communication with the NBA and its outside counsel retained to lead the NBA's oversight function. Mark Cuban, proprietor of the team, was questioned directly by NBA Counsel on at least two separate occasions.[166]

The section of the investigative report about management issues showed that before this investigation, Cuban was rarely in the Mavericks' business office. Instead, Cuban spent most of his time managing the basketball operations division, which until the fall of 2017 was located three miles from the business office. Cuban's involvement in business operations was primarily through email. On the one hand, Cuban's absence indicated that he likely had no idea what was happening in the business divisions, so he wasn't complicit

---

165 "The Report of the Independent Investigation of Dallas Basketball Limited." Courthouse News. September 19, 2018.
166 Ibid.

in any of the egregious and morally corrupt behavior at the subject of the investigations.[167]

On the other hand, leaders need to be around their people to lead properly. Cuban acknowledged in his interview, "You have to be around the culture to see the culture; I learned the hard way." Because he primarily gave direction remotely and didn't have scheduled meetings with management or senior staff, he simply wasn't "around the culture." As the investigative team aptly stated, "his absence from the business office kept him from appreciating either the full scope of the misconduct at the company or the workplace culture at the business office."[168]

A lot went wrong with the Mavericks, which begs the question: how can you do right by your people and correct course when things have steered in the wrong direction? What can we learn from leaders who admit their mistakes and then work to fix them? There is power in admitting and learning from your mistakes, which is why the Mavericks make an excellent case study on how to approach diversity.

First, Cuban took full ownership. He apologized profusely for the toxic culture festering under his watch. He took ownership, publicly stating what he and the organization did wrong, what they learned, and how they would prevent a repeat of the same mistakes.

---

167 Ibid.
168 Ibid.

Next, he solidified the new diverse and inclusive direction the organization would be taking and sought out industry experts who knew how to ask the right questions and provide strong solutions. His first move? He brought on Cynthia Marshall ("Cynt") to be the new CEO of the organization.

Maybe "brought on" isn't the right phrase. It might be more accurate to say that he asked, and she accepted.

When Cuban first called her, Cynt didn't even know who he was. "Who's that?" Cynt recalls asking her husband when he told her Mark Cuban was calling for her.[169] Cuban had called her because he hoped that Cynt, an expert in diversity and inclusion, and former chief diversity officer at AT&T, could turn things around. Within 100 days, Cynt, the first female African American CEO in the league, did exactly that.[170]

"I walked into a bad culture," Cynt reported. "I walked into a place where the women were not valued and treated the way I would like to see them treated. Frankly, I think we had a problem with how we respected and treated people of color. It wasn't a very diverse and inclusive environment when I got there. And so we needed to do some things."[171]

Cynt saw that the culture wasn't one where women felt they could thrive, so she began changing the climate from the

169 Matt Goodman, "Meet Cynt Marshall, the Woman Who Mark Cuban Hopes Can Fix the Mavericks' Culture." D Magazine. February 26, 2018.

170 Jon Wertheim and Jessica Luther, "Exclusive: Inside the Corrosive Workplace Culture of the Dallas Mavericks," Sports Illustrated, February 20, 2018.

171 Poppy Harlow, host, "Cynthia Marshall: Rebuilding the Dallas Mavericks," September 30, 2019, in Boss Files, podcast audio, 53:00.

inside out. The organization's mission was to provide both fans and employees with the best experience possible, so Cynt began talking to each employee and asked them about their experiences and what they wanted to see changed.

To implement the changes, Cynt's first 100 days consisted of hiring a new chief ethics and compliance officer, instituting a zero-tolerance policy for workplace misconduct, and implementing mandatory anti-harassment, respect, and discrimination training for all employees, including people on the basketball side. Employees also gained access to a hotline to report any inappropriate behavior toward themselves or others.

Then, Cynt created a women's playbook designed to empower, uplift, and retain female employees by making sure they felt respected, heard, and valued. Providing mentorship opportunities to improve diversity was a primary step.[172]

She also took a look at the leadership at the Mavericks, which was composed entirely of white men. Cynt changed all of that. As of Fall 2019, 50 percent of the Mavs' leaders were women, and 47 percent were people of color.[173]

Simply hiring more women wasn't enough, though. The previous culture had left female employees skeptical and worried, so she also created employee resource groups that are open to everyone:

---

172 "The Report of the Independent Investigation of Dallas Basketball Limited, "Courthouse News. September 19, 2018.

173 Ibid.

"As women in this organization, what are we all about as women as a unit but also as individuals? What are we about every day? What do we bring in here every day? What value do we add? I'm trying to get them to see they do add value... The beauty of this is the men are all over this. They come to ERG meetings. These men have mothers, wives, daughters, and THEY WANT THIS INCLUSIVE ENVIRONMENT."[174] -CYNT MARSHALL

Cuban noticed a huge difference in the Mavericks organization after Cynt took over. "She has completely revolutionized the culture of the business side of the Mavs," Cuban said. "Her imprint is in every part of the business. We have improved in every facet, and she deserves the credit."[175]

Cynt emphasizes the importance of speaking up and being clear about what you stand for and what you stand against. If you believe in equity, equality, and justice, say so. Take a stand and be heard and make it okay for everyone else in your organization to do the same.

SPEAK UP

Cynt's comment about speaking up and taking a stand isn't just a message for leadership. This message applies to all of us, both in and out of work. We will all need an ally at some

---

174 Deborah Ferguson, "Mavs CEO Celebrates Completion of 100-Day Plan to Change Workplace Culture," NBC Dallas-Fort Worth, August 17, 2018.

175 Brad Townsend, "One Year Later: How the Mavs' Culture Transformed from 'Corrosive' to Inclusive," The Dallas Morning News, September 18, 2019.

point, and we should all strive to speak up and be an ally for others, not despite our differences, but because of them.

When I was a senior in high school, I left a function at our Hindu temple in Parma, Ohio, and decided to stop by the local mall to pick up an Orange Julius from the food court. As I entered the mall wearing my Indian *salwar kameez,* I walked past a crowd of teens hovering nearby. I could hear a couple of people snickering and cackling about how it would be hilarious watching me order because I probably couldn't understand English or read the menu. I could feel their eyes on me. I felt my body tense up, suddenly conscious of the physical space I was taking up in the food court, acutely aware of the distance between them and me, and between myself and the exit. I got my orange and, surprisingly, over-filled drink. When I inserted the straw, an orange avalanche started spilling over onto my hands. Grateful for the distraction, I took my time grabbing napkins and cleaning up because I wanted to wait until the crew of teens left so I wouldn't have to walk past them again.

When I finally ventured out to the parking lot, a gray sedan screeched to a stop next to me. "Go back to your country, you dirty immigrant!" the driver screamed. My stomach dropped—the scream came from one of the guys from the food court. I tried to ignore him, keeping my gaze on my own car, but he kept pulling up right next to me, trying to get me to react. I could barely walk straight without shaking. The sun was blazing down on me. My heart was pounding. My legs felt like Jello as I silently commanded them to keep walking. The teen kept screaming profanities at me, at one point threatening to run me over. I started to fear for my safety.

I felt a bolt of electricity course through my body. This was the first time I felt unadulterated terror.

It's weird how time can slow down when you're truly terrified. I started thinking about how my little sister needed me and how my older brother would miss me. For some reason, I started laughing maniacally at my morbid realization about middle kids: we could exit our families without disrupting anyone's role. If the oldest child disappears, the middle kid suddenly becomes the oldest. But if the middle child disappears? No one's title really changes. I snapped back to the present as I heard the loud sounds of a guy who had just jumped out of his pickup truck. He was rushing toward me. I can't remember exactly what his tank top said, but it had a picture of an American flag on it. He had a tattoo on his face that looked like a bunch of tiny arrows forming some sort of jigsaw puzzle. He reeked of cigarette smoke. He suddenly swung his arms out. I was sure he was about to hit me. I braced myself to get the wind knocked out of me, but what happened next wasn't what I expected.

"Get the HELL out of here, you little prick, before I kick your sorry racist ass down to Cincinnati!" he yelled, arms swinging angrily toward the racist driver. He started swinging at the back of the gray sedan with such force that I thought the teen's trunk was going to end up in the front seat.

Needless to say, he scared the racist off. I had completely misjudged what an ally should and would look like, and when and where he would appear. This was a lesson for me to check my own biases because someone I had mistaken for a threat stood up for me when I needed it most, not even expecting a "thank you" in return, because he slipped away before I could catch his name.

We will all have our "parking lot" moments within the workplace, sometimes needing to have an ally and sometimes needing to be one. Allyship comes in many forms, and luckily, most of them don't involve punching the back of someone's car. Here are some simple tips you can promote diversity through allyship at work:

- Show respect and establish values. Under Cynt's leadership, the Dallas Mavericks rolled out a "Respect in the Workplace" policy, focusing on a zero-tolerance and values-based employment workplace. Cynt and her team also came up with a new code of conduct, which encompassed the foundation of the organization's identity and emphasized things like teamwork, safety, respect, and authenticity.[176] You can create your own policies about respect. In a nutshell, the goal is to treat all people from all walks of life with baseline respect. It's the fundamental ABCs of humanity we all learn as kindergarteners but somehow forget over the years.
- Understand and champion different types of diversity. Gender and race are often the first types of diversity that come to mind, but diversity doesn't stop there. Things like disability status, age, military/veteran status, religion, background, familial status, and educational background are just a few other areas companies need to consider if they want to be inclusive in their diversity.

---

176 Cynt Marshall, *Cynt Marshall to Anne*. Letter. From Rack CDN. Accessed September 5, 2020.

- Be an ally by having the CEO actively demand diversity. When Cynt took the reins as CEO of the Mavericks, one of the first things she did was recognize and emphasize the importance of diversity in every level of the organization.[177] Though it's encouraging to see so many organizations creating new job positions based around diversity, it's equally important to have these positions report directly to the CEO. Think about it. A diversity officer who reports to general counsel will be focused on legal issues, while a diversity officer reporting to marketing will be thinking about social media and protecting its brand. To fully penetrate every level of the organization and be a true ally of diversity, the CEO needs to be on board. They need to give diversity directors the power to do the messy work of examining the company's metrics for compensation, hiring, retention, and promotions.[178]
- Is your hiring process biased? Fix it.[179] The first step to correct a biased hiring process is by looking at your job descriptions. Studies show that men will apply for a job if they meet even 60 percent of the qualifications, but women will only apply when they meet 100 percent of them, so, focus on what a candidate will be expected to achieve, say, a month, six months, and a year into the job.[180] It's also important to look at who is conducting the interviewing. Does the interviewing panel reflect the same diversity it seeks? The interviewers are as important

---

177 Ibid.

178 Haley Draznin, "The Dallas Mavericks Were Plagued by a Toxic Culture. She is Turning it Around." CNN Business, November 19, 2019.

179 "How We Make Textio," Textio, accessed August 8, 2020.

180 Tara Sophia Mohr, "Why Women Don't Apply for Jobs Unless They're 100% Qualified." Harvard Business Review. August 25, 2014.

as the interviewee, partly because a diverse interviewing panel is less likely to reject a candidate because of a lack of "culture fit." If you're part of an interviewing panel and you are leaning toward rejecting a candidate because of a gut feeling or lack of a culture fit, unconscious biases may be seeping in.[181] Finally, when you hire for a job, look past the shiny objects (like an Ivy League education). Some jobs require a particular degree, but many wildly successful leaders like Bill Gates, Mark Zuckerberg, and Richard Branson made it to where they are without traditional schooling credentials. Through a process called psychometric assessments, you can bypass the importance of say, a GPA, and shift the focus to a collection of personality traits that have been identified as predictive of career longevity and success.[182]

TELL YOUR DIVERSITY STORY

While creating and enforcing diversity policies are important, equally important is the practice of having real conversations about diversity and how we can improve it at our organizations. When we relay stories about our diversity, we relay emotion and let people know who we are as employees, friends, daughters, spouses, or advocates. We start thinking, "Hmm, I can see myself in that position…"

Stories connect us. They persuade us. And they motivate us. Science backs this up. Have you ever watched a show on tv where you feel like you are in the character's world?

---

181 Leah Knobler, "Diversity and Inclusion at Help Scout: 2018 Update," Help Scout, August 16, 2018.

182 "Reach for the Stars: Realizing the Potential of America's Hidden Talent Pool." Opportunity at Work. March 2020.

Your heart might start pounding, or tears might start welling up in your eyes. You know that the events aren't actually happening to you, but you feel like they are because you are so engaged. According to Professor of Psychology and Neuroscience Uri Hasson, as you hear someone's story, your brain waves actually start synchronizing with the storyteller's.[183]

When Uri and his research team monitored the brain activity in two people, one person told a story and the other listened. Then, something amazing happened: they found that the greater the listener's comprehension, the more closely the brain wave patterns mirrored those of the storyteller.[184]

Plenty of data related to diverse workforces' business imperatives is all over the Internet, and I even scattered a solid dozen citations about it earlier in the book. Why? Because it's solid data. But here's the thing: solid data won't stick the way a personal story does. You might not remember the facts of a 20-page PowerPoint presentation, but you'll remember how you felt when you heard a story from a person who cared enough to tell it.

For organizations trying to make meaningful diversity impact, stories can help. They can be tools to clarify how employees experience work and where they feel blocked by biases or limitations. They allow you to take that information and strengthen the connective tissue of your organization.

---

183 Greg Stephens et al., "Speaker- Listener Neural Coupling Underlies Successful Communication." Proceedings of the National Academy of Sciences of the United States of America 107, 32 (August 2010): 14425-30.

184 Elena Renken, "How Stories Connect And Persuade Us: Unleashing The Brain Power of Narrative." NPR. April 11, 2020.

When a single parent tells you that she doesn't know how she will move up in her organization if she is constantly ostracized for leaving work to pick up her child, or a developer tells you that he was denied a promotion because of his thick accent, or a Black marketing manager shares that he wasn't even considered for a position because of his lack of Ivy League education, we need to listen.

We need to start speaking up about our experiences. What is it about work interactions, or the lack thereof, that keeps you up at night? What are people thinking and feeling about current events happening around them? How are these events impacting your mindset, your work, and your life? Who has your back? Whose back do you have? Who is consistently being left out in the cold?

Having courageous conversations allows people to speak up and listen at an early stage. Once you start asking these questions and hearing people's responses, you may become aware of unconscious biases that have crept into your organization, preventing you from effectively diversifying your teams. By listening to these stories, we broaden and diversify our circles. Our community starts to widen, and the issues that once seemed to be "their" problems become "our" fights.

Going back to the Dallas Mavericks, Cynt Marshall began to speak openly about her experiences, good and bad, and realized that many of her colleagues shared common experiences. She was vulnerable and shared many facets of her life: from being poor to having four miscarriages to her daughter dying, to living through stage 3 colon cancer. In her childhood, her dad once struck her so hard that her nose was broken. The relationship was so bad that the family had to leave the house. When they returned home, everything was gone except for a mattress.[185]

"He said we'd be hookers on the street without him," Marshall, who was 15 at the time, reported. "My mom said at 15 years old I responded, 'No, we're going to be the first in the family to go to college'… and that I was going to be the president of something one day."[186]

Cynt opened herself up, showing not just her executive side but her human side. In sharing the many diverse sides of herself, she also made it okay for others around her to share their multi-faceted and diverse selves. This sharing of stories leads to communication and strengthening of relationships. In Cynt's own words, "Use these new relationships as an opportunity to sharpen perspectives about other races, genders, cultures, and experiences, and to challenge your beliefs."[187]

Cynt is a powerful example of how authentic communication and storytelling can create a sense of community and belonging to build the compassionate culture we need. Here are some ways to use storytelling and the power of listening to impact diversity at work:

---

185 Jade Scipioni, "Dallas Mavericks CEO to leaders: 'This is Our Moment. Don't Miss It,'" CNBC, last modified June 18, 2020.

186 Jerry Bembry, "Mavericks' Cynthia Marshall: 'I Want to Do it For the Sisterhood,'" The Undefeated, February 27, 2018.

187 Jade Scipioni, "Dallas Mavericks CEO to leaders: 'This is Our Moment. Don't Miss It,'" CNBC, last modified June 18, 2020.

- Listen. Ask people what they need at work and what challenges they face. Follow up with employees and ask how they are doing, whether they need a mentor, sponsor, or new project opportunity to move them forward. At the Mavericks, Cynt did one-on-ones with each employee and gave them each a chance to voice their concerns and get to know each other as parents, children, spouses, friends, and advocates. She listened to why people left the organization and listened to stories about why people stayed to cultivate the organization's positive cultural attributes.

- Implement employee resource groups. At the Mavericks, Cynt launched several employee resource groups (ERGs) to learn about diversity and give people a safe space to talk, learn, and change. Start and fund ERGs with large enough budgets to compensate speakers, workshops, training, and events. At last check, the Mavericks had ERGS for women, Black employees, and working parents.[188] For your own organization, you can consider ERGs around a myriad of different types of diversity: disabilities, remote workers, Black employees, Millennials... the list is limitless and can be catered to the needs of your own employees.

REINFORCE DIVERSITY USING LEADERS

Everyone has felt like an outsider at some point in their life, and Cynt is no exception.

---

188 Cynt Marshall, *Cynt Marshall to Anne*. Letter. From Rack CDN. Accessed September 5, 2020.

Cynt recalls her experiences with code-switching, which is when you shift the language you use or the way you express yourself in your conversations. It's a way for minorities to adapt to a given environment when they feel alienated or uncomfortable.

"I tried to look the conservative way my colleagues looked," Cynt recalled.[189] As a professional, she was once told she was too "ethnic" because she wore braids and bright red heels. She switched to "normal" shoes and always regretted it. "Stand your ground and be your authentic self," she told her audience at a 2015 Berkeley Women's Empowerment Day.[190]

Sharing leadership stories helps us break free from the comfortable homogeneous environments many of us put ourselves in. The truth is that diversity in the workplace is the best option, but that doesn't mean it's the easiest option. There's no question that diverse workplaces can cause friction and conflict at first. Creating and managing multi-dimensional teams takes work. It means we all have to learn to be more aware of our biases and think about how we approach people and situations. When leaders start sharing their own journeys, obstacles, fears, regrets, and comebacks, they make it okay to stumble, question, and change. They make it okay to be human at work.

---

189 Jade Scipioni, "From the First Black Cheerleader at Berkeley Making History as Mavericks CEO: How Cynt Marshall Did It." CNBC. February 21, 2020.

190 Kelly Dunleavy O'Mara, "Always a Maverick: Cynthia Marshall Made Her Mark Before Dallas." UC Berkeley. September 28, 2018.

Cynt's bio might tell us what she does, but her stories told people who she is. Vulnerability is one tool a leader can use to celebrate their own diversity story and thereby open the communication channels to get the organization to do the same, one story at a time.

REMOTE WORK: DIVERSITY AT A DISTANCE

How can a CEO of an NBA team, or any other organization, promote diversity from a distance? There are a couple of different ways to approach this issue, particularly in light of the 2020 COVID-19 pandemic, which left many people unable to work simply because remote work wasn't available or possible.

The first approach to diversity at a distance is from an immediate short-term perspective. When the NBA season was abruptly postponed in March of 2020, many hourly stadium workers making minimum wage (parking attendants, security, concessions, and housekeeping, to name a few) were left in financial limbo.

Randi Trent is a server at the Wells Fargo Center, where the Philadelphia 76ers basketball team plays. "I've worked at the stadium for the past 19 years. I love my job. My whole income revolves around Philadelphia sports. When a team goes to the playoffs, I make more money. Now that the NBA shut down, my income has dropped to zero."[191]

---

191 Sam Yip, "'Everything Went to Hell': Stadium Workers on the US Sports Shutdown." The Guardian. March 24, 2020.

In light of similar stories within their own team, Mark Cuban and the Mavericks, along with American Airlines and Chimes leadership, made arrangements to pay its own hourly workers for at least six home games.[192]

The short-term approach to diversity from a distance, then, is about making sure you take care of your employees in emergencies like a pandemic, particularly for those who may be living paycheck to paycheck. Many hourly workers come from diverse backgrounds, races, origins, and ethnicities, and their rich array of perspectives makes in-person sports experiences what they are.

We also know of a second way to promote diversity from a distance, one with a slightly longer lens in view. Before the 2020 COVID-19 pandemic, many companies allowed at least partial remote work. In the past several months, the number of remote workers, hybrid environments, and distributed workforces has surged. Successfully attracting a diverse workforce has never been more critical for employers, especially for companies hoping to attract the best and brightest new workers. Millennials and Gen Z'ers are especially interested in diversity. One survey finds that 83 percent of Gen Z candidates look for diversity and inclusion as an important part of their job search.[193]

As more and more companies start embracing remote work, we need to ask ourselves: what's the point of recruiting the

192 Doyle Rader, "Dallas Mavericks Pledge to Pay Arena Staff for Six Postponed Home Games." Forbes. March 13, 2020.
193 "Monster's 2020 State of the Candidate Survey Highlights." Monster. Accessed August 7, 2020.

best talent if they can't see themselves thriving at your organization? What are the expenses, both emotional and financial, of someone who already had their bags packed upon arrival? For example, if we promote diversity, but we can't overcome accessibility challenges for our disabled employees and don't have adequate equipment to accommodate them remotely, what kind of message are we sending?

Promoting diversity in a remote workplace is critical, especially because many people have not and may never meet in person. They need to know that their voices will be heard and that they will matter.

Here's a case in point. My dad is a semi-retired organic chemist who immigrated from India several decades ago. He recollected a story about being a new employee at his company when he was younger. There was a brainstorming session for an ambitious new project. The president had scheduled an audio recording so everyone's suggestions could be recorded, but every time my dad tried to speak, someone would interrupt and talk over him. The president noticed. After the meeting, the president invited my dad into his office and asked the secretary to record his project perspectives. From that point on, my dad knew that diversity was valued, that his opinions mattered, and that HE mattered.

As new remote employees start onboarding and joining existing teams of people who already know each other, we can all take my dad's advice on promoting diversity: prioritize the people in your organization and help them be heard.

TO SUM UP:

The saying that diversity equals strength isn't just a PR tag line. It's the truth and reminds me of this paradox from my college days in Ohio. I used to love arguing with my philosophy professor after class. One of our favorite conversations was about the immovable force paradox, which asks the question: "Can an unstoppable force move an immovable object?" The paradox is flawed, the argument goes, because an unstoppable force, to become unstoppable, has to possess infinite energy. On the other hand, an immovable object is not submissive to any force of any size or magnitude, so both declarations can't be true at the same time.

Bringing this paradox back to diversity, I've sometimes been told that having an all-White, all older male leadership team is just how it is. The homogeneity is tradition. It's entrenched. It's basically an immovable object.

Here's my issue with that logic. Homogeneity is not a fixed barrier. It's something we choose. It's something we create. It's also something we can change.

We can use our voices, our money, our power, our passion, our platforms, and our common humanity to change the status quo of what our organizations look like from the outside, as well as what they feel like from the inside. Cynthia Marshall has done it. Mark Cuban has done it. Countless others have done it. Homogeneity is not fixed but it is *fixable*. Just look at the demographics of the United States. By

2050, there will be no clear ethnic or racial majority in the United States.[194] Do you know what that tells us?

Homogeneity has *never* been an immovable object. Diversity is the **unstoppable force.**

---

194 "By 2050 There Will be No Clear Racial or Ethnic Majority in our Nation." Center for American Progress, April 2012. "

CHAPTER NINE

HOW TO IMPROVE INCLUSION

———

"Urging an organization to be inclusive is not an attack. It's progress."

— DASHANNE STOKES[195]

What is pain? One common definition is that it's a warning signal that something is wrong or damaged. It's not just people who feel pain. Companies feel it. Even cars feel it.

After I graduated law school, I moved to Chicago with two suitcases, a houseplant, and my gray Subaru Loyale. The car had always been comfortable and dependable. But for the past several months, I had been noticing a strange squealing noise from the front of the car that sounded like a mouse with its tail stuck under a fence post. I learned that turning

---

195 "Dashanne Stokes Quotes," Dashannestokes.com, accessed August 8, 2020.

up the volume on my radio would drown out the noise. When the car's repeated squeals went unaddressed, it started warning me with a flickering red light whenever I started the car. I had neither the time nor the inclination to take a day off work and sit at the dealership all day, so I did what any unreasonable and illogical person would do: I ignored it and covered the warning light with duct tape.

The frequency of the car's warnings started to increase, but I learned that if I just turned off the ignition and waited for a few minutes, the car would relent on its repeated attempts to warn me. I thought the silence meant I had things under control.

A couple of months later, I was driving on I-55 toward Midway Airport. Bruce Springsteen was playing on the radio, and the heat was blasting through the vents when suddenly my car's speed dropped from 65mph to zero. It felt like someone had forcefully yanked an appliance from its power source. The steering wheel locked. The alternator belt snapped, and my engine died in the middle of the highway. If it wasn't for the quick judgment of the drivers behind me, I probably wouldn't have survived. When I called my parents later that evening, I cried emphatically, "I'm in disbelief. I have no idea how this could have happened!"

Let's be real; that's hardly the truth. My car had over 89,000 miles on it when the incident occurred. I couldn't remember the last time I had my car inspected. The squealing noises and the flashing lights were symptoms that I repeatedly ignored, occasionally masking them with loud music or duct tape.

There was a much larger problem at hand, but I just looked the other way until it became nearly catastrophic.

Like me, many people have a bad habit of addressing symptoms instead of the underlying problems. It can't be emphasized strongly enough that symptoms are an indicator that something is not right. My story was about a car, but it could just as easily apply to our workplaces.

If your organization is focused on diverse recruiting but lacks an inclusive environment, something is not right. If there's a disproportionately high attrition rate in middle management with underrepresented groups, with leadership teams all looking the same, something is not right. If you have a pile of exit interviews where employees are reporting that they left because they didn't feel welcome, something is not right.

Too many companies ignore their problems by "plugging the hole" with some new hires or a quick training workshop. They don't do the hard work of looking under the proverbial hood and having difficult conversations to see what's really happening at the organization. They don't take the time to really get to know their people. They don't embrace and celebrate the diversity of ideas, perspectives, and cultures. Instead of helping people stay engaged while they are still with the company, they try to do damage control once ex-employees start sharing their horror stories on Glassdoor or LinkedIn. They do the equivalent of turning up the radio volume or slapping duct tape over the warning light.

To better understand workers' experiences and challenges, we need to have real conversations about inclusion, wellbeing, and connection at work. We need to do "maintenance" checks of our organizations and assess a company's people and processes, which means we need people to start taking care of themselves and each other—not just when someone is watching, but all the time.

If we ignore the warning signals and treat our organizations like I treated my Subaru, we may one day find ourselves broken down on the side of the road, and that's if we're lucky. If we're not so lucky? Well, we may just get run over.

SHOW YOUR HUMANITY

As leaders and employees, we should aim to listen to each other a little more and embrace different ideas from different people. Once we're more open to different perspectives, we will also learn that there is more than one way to live, and more than one right way to think and act. Hearing a wide range of perspectives and experiences helps us relate to other people. It creates empathy.

Empathy happens when we recognize and understand other people's feelings and see what it's like to be in their shoes. It's an often overlooked but critical skill in today's workplace. Bill Gates puts it this way: "If we have optimism, but we don't have empathy, then it doesn't matter how much we master the secrets of science. We're not really solving problems; we're just working on puzzles."[196]

---

196 Bill Gates and Melinda Gates, "2014 Commencement Address," June 15, 2014, Stanford University, Stanford, CA.

One real-life example of empathy in action is Attorney, Author, and Addiction Recovery Advocate, Brian Cuban.

I first met Brian when he keynoted the Commission on Lawyer Assistance Program Conference in Austin in 2019. Brian is a Dallas-based attorney who has been in long-term recovery from alcohol, cocaine, and bulimia since 2007. He is also the younger brother of Dallas Mavericks owner and Shark Tank investor Mark Cuban.

On the evening of the keynote, I was expecting a pretty formal talk about lawyer assistance needs. What I heard instead was a raw and vulnerable account of how Brian's mental health issues and addiction tore his career, relationships, and life apart, and how he found his way to recovery and healing.

He recounted some personal stories, and a particular incident about being bullied as a child almost had me in tears. It involved a pair of disco pants, a sidewalk, and some cruel kids. So many decades later, he says he can still point out the exact spot on the Pittsburgh sidewalk where his dignity and disco pants were shredded. The evening I first met Brian, I was envious of his ability to unmask some of his most painful memories, with nothing but a wooden podium to protect him from the rest of the room.

I've always struggled to show authentic vulnerability, but that night, the openness was contagious. By the end of the talk, colleagues at my dinner table were openly recounting their own childhood experiences. The conversation took a decidedly deeper and more meaningful tone as we realized we had a lot more in common than our legal backgrounds.

During the talk, Brian spoke about empathy and compassion, and the value of simply asking someone how they're doing. Despite the belief that checking in on someone can be outside our comfort zone because it seems intrusive, Brian encouraged people to ask anyways. It's how compassion is built. On his website, Brian expands on that thought:

> "We are people. We have stories. We get depressed. We stress. We cry. We laugh. We grieve. We are all more than our struggle, but when we look at our peers, we are often uncomfortable acknowledging that struggle, let alone a person with a life story.........How do we, as a profession, foster a culture of compassion toward each other when we are often at each other's throats. A culture of community in which we both take care of ourselves and our colleagues. It is through a compassionate community."[197]

Brian's philosophy of building compassionate communities is in line with diversity strategist Joel Brown, who talks about overcoming "the empathy gap," which exists when a person's unconscious biases inhibit them from truly empathizing with another person who differs from their own identity, background, beliefs or experiences. When you have an empathy gap, you tend to view a person (or group of people) abstractly, and you end up dehumanizing their experiences.[198] How do you overcome the empathy gap? By making a concerted effort. By asking people how they are and listening to their response.

---

197 Brian Cuban, "Creating Compassionate Community in the Legal Profession," Briancuban.com, February 21, 2020.

198 Joel Brown, The Diversity Collegium. Accessed September 6, 2020.

As I left the dinner that night, I started thinking about how people are like icebergs: what we show the world can be pretty limited. So many aspects of ourself dwell silently under the waterline. When a courageous person openly shares their struggles and uncertainties, it has a ripple effect of encouraging everyone around them to share more of their own authentic selves. We start to uncover our commonalities and learn how to relate to people who have struggles that vary from our own. By sharing our own truths, we also develop empathy and compassion for other people. Organizations can follow this process by having "Courageous Conversations," where employees of all backgrounds talk about difficult issues. Yes, the conversations can get heated, and they can get uncomfortable. But it's critical to building the compassionate communities Brian advocates.[199]

Brian points to something important in his talks: empathy isn't just about connecting to an experience. It's about connecting to the emotions under that experience. It takes patience and kindness to walk over to someone else's life landscape, look down, and see a situation from their perspective. Writer and speaker Brene Brown takes a similar approach and says that empathy is a choice to connect with something in yourself that knows that feeling that someone else is feeling.[200]

199 Howard Ross, "Don't Let Divisions Lead to Workplace Dysfunction." SHRM. May 9, 2018.

200 Brené Brown, *The Gifts of Imperfection: Let Go of Who You Think You're Supposed to Be and Embrace Who You Are* (Center City: Hazelden Publishing, 2010),26.

Empathetic listening isn't necessarily about fixing anything. It's not just about the "what"; it's also about the "who" and the "why." It's about paying attention to what someone is saying and how they are feeling and taking the time to understand why. It's about the humane act of reaching out to people who can't or won't reach for you first.

HOW ORGANIZATIONS CAN FOSTER INCLUSION AND BELONGING:

- <u>Try the inside scoop.</u> In *Together*, Former Surgeon General Vivek Murthy talked about the "Inside Scoop," an all-hands meeting designed to strengthen connection. Team members were asked to share non-work-related elements about themselves through pictures for five minutes at each weekly staff meeting. Presenting was an opportunity to share more of their lives, and listening was an opportunity to recognize colleagues in the ways they wished to be seen.[201]

- <u>Open challenge exercise.</u> Have each team member write down or talk about a challenge from the past week, then go around the room and chat openly together about how each person can overcome their obstacles. As people open up about their challenges, you'll start to connect and create a stronger culture.

- <u>Listen more, assume less.</u> In *Talking to Strangers*, Malcolm Gladwell states: "The conviction that we know others better than they know us—and that we may have insights about them they lack (but not vice versa) leads

---

201 Vivek H. Murthy, *Together: The Healing Power of Human Connection in a Sometimes Lonely World* (New York: Harper Wave, 2020), 121-23.

us to talk when we would do well to listen and to be less patient than we ought to be when others express the conviction that they are the ones being misunderstood or judged unfairly."[202] When we confront a stranger or a near stranger that we only know for their position, we often substitute a stereotype for direct experience with that person. And that stereotype is often wrong. Want to know what your team members need? Don't assume. Ask. And make the environment inclusive enough so they feel safe answering.

IMPROVE YOUR POLICIES

In addition to listening compassionately and simply being there, it's important to analyze and adjust non-inclusive workplace policies. Do you remember the childhood saying—"Sticks and stones may break my bones, but words will never hurt me"? Personally, I've never understood that statement. Words don't hurt? Try saying that to someone who has been harassed at work. Words have tremendous power, and so does something else: complete silence.

In 2014, my family tried to rent a home in the DC area. The whole process was extremely dehumanizing and humiliating, leading us to file a discrimination complaint. After two years of pursuing the case on our own, the Attorney General intervened and advocated for our constitutional rights. Eighteen months later, we decided to accept a settlement payout.

---

202 Malcolm Gladwell, *Talking to Strangers: What We Should Know about the People we Don't Know* (New York: Hachette, 2019), 352.

I can't get into extensive details about what happened, and with whom, mostly because I signed a non-disclosure agreement ("NDA") as part of my settlement, which limits me from talking about my discrimination case in any real detail.

NDAs have a pretty wide reach once signed: suddenly, telling your friend why a specific employer or company is awful becomes a bad idea. That Twitter takedown you had planned in your head? No longer an option. An interview with a local news station to prevent a repeat of whatever happened to you? Completely out of the question.

Signing a settlement agreement doesn't mean you're suddenly over the series of incidents that led to the suit. I can tell you that you never "get over" these things. When I filed suit, I wanted someone to answer what I saw as a fundamental violation of my family's rights. I don't regret fighting for myself or my family. But when you embark on a journey like mine, you become a prisoner of your own battle. In my case, taking a settlement was best for my sanity, my family, and my career.

My situation dealt with a rental agreement for housing, but the same situation can come up for the one-third of the US workforce bound by some sort of non-disclosure agreement (NDA).[203]

NDAs are nothing new. Employers can use NDAs for a lot of reasons. They can serve a legitimate purpose in the

---

203 "Non-Disclosure Agreements (NDA's)," Workplace Fairness, accessed August 8, 2020.

workplace in protecting trade secrets or other confidential information like intellectual property or information about a company's clients.

In many cases, though, NDAs are being abused, and people who sign them are not aware of their rights. NDA agreements have grown in both number and scope and have been used to cover up discrimination, harassment, and victimization in just about any imaginable industry.[204]

For every story that has surfaced, many other stories that should be exposed are kept from the public because of NDAs that restrict people from informing the public, seeking justice or recalibrating the culture at a workplace gone awry. According to one study, up to one-third of US workers have signed an NDA. This leads to the question: why do some organizations treat a victim's payoff as a cost of doing business, instead of using the incidents as a wake-up call that a culture overhaul may be needed?[205]

In essence, many NDAs are being used to silence the victim when the real focus should be on eliminating the inappropriate and often illegal actions. The NDAs become muzzles and make it impossible for employees to talk about their issues, either in or out of work. When you tie in the impact of an NDA on employee wellbeing and inclusion, you can see how

204 Jessica Silver-Greenberg and Natalie Kitroeff, "How Bloomberg Buys the Silence of Unhappy Employees," New York Times, last modified March 4, 2020.

205 Hunter Moyler, "Gretchen Carlson Calls on Mike Bloomberg To Free Women From the NDAs They Signed While Working For Him," Newsweek, February 3, 2020.

this could turn anyone into a human pressure cooker with no release valve.

NDAs often prevent employees from speaking up against corporate culture or saying anything that would negatively portray the company and its executives. This inability to speak can directly impact our feelings of inclusion and belonging.

HOW CAN YOU IMPROVE A CULTURE YOU CAN'T EVEN DISCUSS?

Many NDAs also have non-disparagement clauses preventing people from speaking out against an organization's corporate culture, which is problematic. How can we improve an organization's culture if we aren't allowed to talk or even know about it?

For companies seeking to put gender parity and inclusion initiatives into action, narrowly tailoring or eliminating NDAs can be a pathway forward: allowing people to speak signals openly to prospective and existing employees that they have a healthy workplace culture, and that when problems do occur, they will be addressed and not swept silently under the rug.

Part of feeling inclusion and belonging comes from speaking up about any perceptions or incidents of harassment or discrimination. The best way for an organization to tackle the root causes of its problems is to know what they are.

CHANGING THE STATUS QUO

A quiet storm of influential organizations, lawmakers, and change agents are slowly shifting the status quo to end the harmful practice of mandatory NDAs. New Jersey has already passed a law prohibiting enforcement of certain mandatory arbitration and non-disclosure provisions in employment contracts and settlement agreements. California banned forced arbitration as a condition of employment.[206]

Lift Our Voices is a movement advocating for the restriction of mandatory NDAs, confidentiality provisions, and forced arbitration clauses that prevent employees from publicly discussing and disclosing toxic workplace conditions, including sexual harassment and discrimination.[207]

When it comes to NDAs, real change happens from both the top-down and the bottom up. We need leaders to take a serious look at their internal practices and policies and make necessary changes to root out existing problems. When organizations make it clear that harassment and discrimination won't be tolerated or protected by an NDA, the market's best and brightest employees will take notice.[208]

CREATE POLICIES THAT ARE IN LINE WITH AMERICAN VALUES

For all the talk about family values, our company policies don't seem to reflect that. How many companies offer subsidized childcare costs? A disproportionate number of parents

---

206 August W. Heckman et al., "New Jersey Bans Some Non-disclosure and Waiver Provisions," Morgan Lewis, March 25, 2019.

207 Gretchen Carlson, "It's time to Lift Our Voices," accessed August 8, 2020.

208 "Home." The Purple Campaign. Accessed September 6, 2020.

are being priced out of the workforce—the costs of staying in are just too high.[209] Employees are assets to be appreciated, not costs to be minimized.

At the end of the day, every business is about its people. If employees aren't being treated fairly and don't feel safe enough to report problems when they occur, they will eventually leave. Creating, revising, and updating our policies and practices is a key step in the inclusion journey, and that's applicable for both in-person and remote workers.

INCLUSION IN A REMOTE/DISTRIBUTED SETTING

A manager's job is simple, though not always easy: create a work environment where everyone can do their best work. Being in a distributed workforce doesn't negate a manager's responsibility. In a remote setting, it's more important than ever that managers are communicating with their teams.

When remote teams are disengaged, it's often because the manager dropped the ball. In one study, a fourth of virtual teams were inefficient because of poor management.[210] Successful managers regularly communicate with their employees and make sure they know what's happening in the organization and have the tools they need to succeed.

Remote workers face several unique challenges. First, they are more likely to feel isolated, lonely, and depressed because they have less human contact than your other employees.

---

209 E. W., "What's Holding Women Back?" The Economist, January 23, 2015.
210 Keith Ferrazzi, "Getting Virtual Teams Right," Harvard Business Review, December 2014.

Second, they have more distractions around them like noisy kids arguing in the other room. Third, although their intention behind working remotely might have been to have more flexibility, they often end up losing track of time and working around the clock. When you're in an office, you have a more defined workday because you see people coming and going at some point each day.

Whenever there's a dearth of communication across a distributed workplace, people fill that void with assumptions about what's happening or not happening in the business. They can feel really uneasy or disconnected about the business. Consistent communication—and never leaving remote employees to feel like they are on an island is critical.

Here are some tips for increasing inclusion and belonging for your remote workers or distributed workforce:

- Create an employee manual. Remote workers are often onboarding and starting new jobs without having ever met their colleagues in person. To help coworkers understand each other's work and communication style, individuals can prepare their own "user manuals" that explain things like the conditions they like to work in, the times/hours they work best, the best way to communicate with them (text, Slack, phone, Zoom, etc.), how they learn best, things they typically struggle with, things they can help others with, and anything else that helps paint a picture of how to be your best self. Understanding ourselves leads to a better understanding of others, and a better appreciation of differences. It's a great onboarding tool.

- <u>Hold more effective meetings.</u> An employee's daily experiences with coworkers are more telling about a workplace's inclusiveness than anything else. Some key actions you can take include allowing each person a designated time to talk on conference calls, rotating meeting times to accommodate international workers, and distributing meeting materials in advance to provide people ample time to review the materials and offer questions and feedback.

- <u>Understand that harassment and exclusion still happen in remote work.</u> Ally Coll and Shea Holman of the *Purple Campaign* remind us that workplace harassment doesn't disappear when employees stop physically working alongside coworkers in brick and mortar locations.[211] In fact, workers who work in isolated spaces, including domestic care, hotels, and agricultural workers, are more likely to experience harassment.[212] We need to pay attention to who we hear from and who we aren't, Coll states, since employees often withdraw after being harassed.[213] Apps like AllVoices allow employees, contractors, and vendors to report issues to companies anonymously. Ally reiterates that employers can still conduct thorough investigations in remote climates and still keep their main focus on stopping improper conduct. Diversity and inclusion play a big part in harassment prevention- leveraging diversity and inclusion efforts can lower harassment complaints

211 Ally Coll and Shea Holman, "Steps to Maintain Workplace Equality During the Pandemic," Law360, April 27, 2020.

212 Elyse Shaw et al., "Sexual Harassment and Assault at Work: Understanding the Costs." Institute for Women's Policy Research. October 2018.

213 Robyn Swirling, "Sexual Harassment Still Happens When You Work from Home During a Pandemic," Medium, March 17, 2020.

because people who feel heard, included, and valued are less likely to file complaints.

Work culture is, and always will be, important—regardless of whether employees are in the office or work remotely.[214] Having a true inclusion culture where every voice matters is not a perk—it's a necessity for every organization.

INDIVIDUAL RESPONSIBILITIES FOR AN INCLUSIVE WORKPLACE

We've covered a bit of what companies can do for us and what we can do for other people to promote inclusion, but what about the things we can do for ourselves? We can start by looking deeper into some of our own common beliefs, statements, and actions.

- Don't ignore someone's identity, and don't ignore your own. "I don't see color." How many of us have said or heard that comment before? I've heard it in the context of well-intentioned people trying to say that everyone is equal or that if they themselves don't make race an issue, no one else will. The problem with this logic is that one person saying they don't judge based on race doesn't mean the rest of the world will magically follow suit, and ignoring a large part of a person's identity can make people feel unheard and unseen.
- Check your own biases. We all have biases. Some biases are personal, and others are societal. One of my personal

214 "Chart of Risk Factors for Harassment and Responsive Strategies," US Equal Employment Opportunity Commission, accessed August 8, 2020.

biases I shared earlier was about the man with the face tattoo who saved me in the Parma, Ohio parking lot. I had a personal bias against people with tattoos, assuming they were somehow menacing based on misguided notions.

On the other hand, societal biases are things we hear and learn about through our communities and surroundings, and they are things we either adapt or reject. Earlier in the book, I explained what an Indian biodata was, which is essentially a résumé to rank your marriage potential. High up on that list of priority items if you're female? Skin color. Colorism is big business in India and has long been a part of many Asian narratives. Darker-skinned women face discrimination at school, at work, and especially in dating. Until recently, Shaadi.com, an Indian matchmaking site, had a filter to weed out dark-skinned prospects, a preposterous feature that wasn't removed until intense backlash in 2020.[215] The good thing about societal biases, if anything, is that we can often see them for what they are and break free of them.

- <u>Adopt a sports mindset.</u> Football coach Bill Curry is known for always mentioning the "miracle of sport." ESPN reporter Richard Lapchick describes the miracle of sport this way:
  "In the huddle, it doesn't matter whether you're Black, white, Middle Eastern, Latino, Asian or Native American. It matters not whether you are Christian, Jewish, Buddhist, Muslim, Sikh, Hindu, or believe in any other religion or no religion. Whether you are young or old,

---

215 Rak Kaur Bilkhu, "Shaadi.com: Dating Site Removes Skin Tone Filter After Backlash." BBC News. June 23, 2020.

*gay or straight, it does not matter whether you are a
rich family or poor family. The team simply cannot win
unless everyone pulls together. Imagine if that power
of sports spread to all institutions and communities
across the globe."*[216]

What is it about sports that makes our differences slide away?
Reid Hoffman, author of the *Alliance,* is on to something
when he says that businesses should be like sports teams.
He says: "Teams win when their members trust each other
enough to prioritize team success over individual success.
The members of a winning team are highly sought after by
other teams, both for the skills they demonstrate and their
ability to help a new team develop a winning idea."[217]

With team sports, every player wants their team members
to do well. Losses happen, but when they do, the team looks
for lessons in defeat. Losses are an opportunity to learn what
went wrong, understand why, and how to prevent it from
happening again. As individuals, we can all try to adopt the
sports mindset of unity and shared purpose where every
player is part of the team.

SUMMING IT UP:
When it comes to inclusion in the workplace, there's a lot
we can do in traditional office settings, hybrid workforces,
and individually. There's a saying in Hindi: "आप क्या बनना

---

216 Richard Lapchick, "How Sports is Helping Orlando Heal." ESPN. June 20,
     2016.
217 Reid Hoffman et al., *The Alliance: Managing Talent in the Networked
     Age.* Boston: Harvard Business Review Press, 2014.

चाहते हैं" which roughly translates to "What do you want to be?"

Who I am and what I show you depends largely on what the workforce encourages and embraces. A truly inclusive workforce will enable me to bring my whole self to work: it will embrace my questions, my struggles, and my wisdom as I learn from my mistakes and continue to evolve. An inclusive workforce will have its foundation in compassionate communities, which will be there for us when we need to be heard. They will lead us through tough conversations and confirm that our complex, multi-layered lives don't make us inadequate. They make us human.

CHAPTER TEN

HOW TO INCREASE INCLUSIVE RECRUITING

"You're not just recruiting employees but are sowing the seeds of your reputation."

-ANONYMOUS

Let's address the chapter heading right away and clear up a common misconception about hiring. The common refrain of "But I don't see race/gender/disability/fill in the blank when hiring" is a bit misguided. First, seeing these characteristics isn't a bad thing. I don't want potential employers to ignore my race, gender, or parental status; these things make me who I am. Second, claiming that *you* don't see those things doesn't change the reality that a large part of the world does see those things and makes biased decisions as a result.

Let's get a bit more specific. What does the data tell us about bias in recruiting, hiring, and promotions? Is there a way to quantify an economic cost of bias? In the fall of 2019, I sought to find out by interviewing Vivienne Ming, theoretical neuroscientist, and founder of data and educational technology company, Socos. When Vivienne was Chief Scientist of HR Tech company Gild, she studied a data set of 122 million professional profiles.[218] She isolated her profiles to focus on over 150,000 people named Joe and over 100,000 people named Jose and found that one simple letter in a name could make a huge difference in a person's job prospects.

Vivienne used the concept of signaling to examine the discrepancy. Vivienne talked about how male peacocks with large tails successfully "signal" to female peacocks that they are more attractive mates. In other words, big tails are the "swipe rights" of the peacock world even though their tails don't really hold any real survival value. The peacock analogy isn't too different from the signaling of Indian "biodatas" (aka marriage résumé), which automatically score you higher if you're a male doctor or a light-skinned woman. These are coveted traits that prove to be absolutely meaningless in determining if a marriage will be successful or not.

Humans often "signal" with their Ivy League educations in a work setting to display their value as a candidate. Vivienne sought to isolate the signals Jose would need compared to Joe to get promoted as a software engineer, starting with college degrees. To be equally likely to get a promotion, someone named Jose would need a master's degree or higher, while

218 Vivienne Ming, "From Cognitive Modeling to Labor Markets" (EdLab Seminar, Vialogues, April 1, 2015).

someone named Joe would need no degree at all for that same promotion.[219]

Numerically, Jose would have to account for six additional years of schooling, along with missed opportunity costs. This would cost Jose $500,000-$1,000,000 over his lifetime. That's a pretty expensive penalty for adding an "S" to the middle of your name and shows the magnitude of implicit or overt bias. Vivienne's research also exposed the following truths:

When given identical résumés, many employers:

- Prefer 'Caucasian' names to 'African American' ones
- Show bias in simple email introductions
- Prefer male names over female names

Bias is real, whether you yourself are guilty of the above preferences or not. We can't afford to overlook or dismiss the immense, diverse talent out there. Diversification in recruiting isn't merely the right thing to do. It's the smart thing to do. Decades of research by sociologists, psychologists, and scientists show that diverse groups (varying races, sexual orientations, genders, and ages) are more creative, productive, and adaptive at problem-solving than homogeneous groups.[220] When we aren't inclusive in hiring, we all lose.

---

219 Vivienne Ming, "The Hidden Tax on Being Different," HR Magazine, November 23, 2016.
220 Katherine W. Phillips, "How Diversity Makes Us Smarter," Scientific American, October 1, 2014.

TOO MANY CEILINGS REMAIN UNSHATTERED

After reading about Vivienne's findings, I thought I'd do a mini experiment of my own since I presumably had at least two traits that employers seemed to find less desirable: I was female and had a non-Caucasian name. The National Bureau of Economic Research has conducted its own study on name bias and found those job applicants with white-sounding names needed to send ten résumés to get a callback. In contrast, Black sounding names would have to send as many as fifteen.[221] As a woman with an Indian name, I sought out to do my own informal experiment.

I used my real name and sent my actual résumé to 10 employers via a job posting site. Then I sent an identical cover letter and résumé to the same 10 employers, changing my name to Andy Peters. I was applying to be a marketing director, something I really have no experience with, so it makes sense that I didn't hear back from most employers. But something interesting happened: one of the employers did email Andy Peters (to a new male sounding email address I had created) and said that "my" lack of experience could be an asset as long as I was willing to learn on my feet.

If I'm honest, learning that my Andy Peters persona might have what it takes to be a marketing director, despite not knowing what a marketing director even does, was exciting.

But reality kicked in when I reminded myself that Anjali, who was real and equally qualified, never heard back. It turns

---

221 David R. Francis, "Employers' Replies to Racial Names." The National Bureau of Economic Research. Accessed September 6, 2020.

out that white-sounding names receive 50 percent more call-backs for interviews than ethnic-sounding names.[222] Double whammy for Anjali: women are often perceived as having lower technical skills.[223] The dismissal of Anjali's résumé may not have been malicious. Still, unconscious bias may have come into play, making it seem that Andy would be more capable than his female counterpart.

The experience took me back to an experience I had with my kids when they were younger. It was a fairly typical summer evening in our neighborhood: I didn't feel like cooking, so I took our three kids to a local pizza place for dinner.

As we squeezed into the booth, a friendly and talkative server took our drink order. As my middle daughter leaned over to grab some napkins, her long springy black curls bounced over her shoulders like hundreds of pressurized mini-mattress springs had suddenly catapulted into freedom.

"Oh my gosh, her hair is so beautiful!" the server gushed as she ran her hands through my daughter's hair. "Where is she from?"

"Where is she from?" might seem like a harmless question, and maybe subtle when it's directed toward a young child. But is that same question harmless when it's directed at an

---

222 Marianne Bertrand, Marianne, and Sendhil Mullainathan, "Are Emily and Greg More Employable than Lakisha and Jamal? A Field Experiment on Labor Market Discrimination," *American Economic Review* 94, no. 4 (September 2004): 991-1013.

223 Sara Ashley O'Brien, "Women Coders, do Better than Men in Gender-Blind Study," CNN Money, February 12, 2016.

adult looking for a job? Is there a cost for looking, sounding, or acting differently from the norm?

It turns out that being "different" comes at a cost. Vivienne Ming has a phrase for the price we pay when we have different hair, different names, different norms, and different backgrounds: it's "a tax of being different." The tax is largely implicit, Vivienne says, and people don't need to be acting maliciously for the tax to be levied.[224]

Vivienne looked at how the tax impacted various groups. Being Black on Wall Street would cost you in the range of $800,000-$1,1000,000. Being a gay man in the UK seems like a relative bargain in comparison, coming in between $65,000-$77,000.

I was interested in learning how much it costs to be a woman. If you're a female software engineer, expect a tax of between $100,000-$300,000 for similar career outcomes.[225] Despite the heavy tax on women, women make up almost half of the US labor force. They outnumber men in earning bachelor's and master's degrees and are on par in getting medical and legal degrees. Sounds great until you look deeper. From corporate boardrooms to Congress, from healthcare companies to the courts, from non-profit organizations to universities, men are much more likely than women to rise to the highest

---

224 Gerson Lehrman Group, Inc., "Neuroscientist Vivienne Ming Discusses 'The Tax on Being Different' And How Big Data Helps Maximize Human Potential," PR Newswire, June 27, 2017.

225 Vivienne Ming, "There is a Tax on Being Different," Financial Times, July 3, 2016.

paying and most prestigious leadership roles.[226] In fact, a Rockefeller Foundation survey found that 1 in 4 Americans believe we will invent time travel before women run half of the Fortune 500 companies.[227]

When it comes to recruiting, employees need to be able to see themselves in leadership. If they can't see themselves eventually moving up, it's likely you won't successfully recruit them. After all, people won't follow a pipeline that won't take them anywhere.

AGEISM IN RECRUITING

Robert Frost wrote about how the afternoon knows what the morning never suspected, which is equally true in the workplace.[228] If the morning was me in my 20s, and the afternoon is the past 20 years, then I should be flying high because I have the benefit of some wisdom and experience, right?

Not exactly.

At the time of publishing, I will be about 45 years old, so when I read that nearly 2 out of 3 workers ages 45 and older have seen or experienced some kind of age discrimination on the job, I thought to myself: when is my time coming?[229]

226 "Barriers and Bias: The Status of Women in Leadership," American Association of University of Women, accessed April 5, 2020.

227 "Women in Leadership: Tackling Corporate Culture from the Top." Rockefeller Foundation. Accessed September 6, 2020.

228 "Robert Frost Quotes." Brainy Quote. Accessed September 6, 2020.

229 Kenneth Terrell, "Age Bias Complaints Rise Among Women and Minorities," AARP, June 28, 2018.

Modern workplaces strive to be inclusive, but age bias creeps in places we don't expect. When it comes to recruiting, words matter. When we see employers talking about GPAs, it's a not-so-subtle way of stating that the employer assumes we are young enough to care, or even remember, how we did in a class several or more decades ago. Age bias can also take a more subtle approach, for example, when a job description refers to being a "digital native" or having "21st-century skills."

More than fifty years after a federal law was passed to give older adults a fair chance to compete for job openings, employers are still posting jobs biased against older applicants.[230] A search conducted by AARP on three major sites (LinkedIn, Monster.com, and Indeed.com) turned up thousands of ads using phrases like "recent college graduate" or "college student."[231] The AARP reports that these terms often appear, even after guidance from the Equal Employment Opportunity Commission (EEOC), stating that they may be violations of federal anti-discrimination law. But older job seekers, who account for more than 20 percent of the nation's workforce, may likely pick up on this language and decide not to apply.[232]

According to many experts, age discrimination in recruiting and hiring has two main causes. First, employers incorrectly assume that older workers will cost them more in

---

230 Ibid.
231 Kimberly Palmer, "10 Things You Should Know About Age Discrimination," AARP, February 20, 2017.
232 David Neumark et al., "Age Discrimination and Hiring Older Workers," Federal Reserve Bank of San Francisco, February 27, 2017.

salary, benefits, or both. Common concerns revolve around healthcare, so let's break this down fairly. Let's use my nearly 80-year-old dad, an organic chemist, as an example. Is it possible that his individual healthcare costs might be higher than mine? Sure, there's no point denying that reality. But those healthcare costs are offset by the fact that many people in his age range are also more likely to carry single or two-person coverage, instead of the family coverage I would seek.

Second, as Facebook CEO Mark Zuckerberg said in 2007, people often may think that "young people are just smarter." Get out of here with that nonsense, Mark. Someone like my dad, and even me, to a lesser extent, have accumulated decades of knowledge and skills. Younger people aren't automatically dumber, nor are they automatically smarter, as evidenced by Mark's failure to acknowledge that baby boomers like Bill Gates and Steve Jobs were the ones who led the tech revolution and made his job possible in the first place.[233]

Age bias hurts workplace culture and hurts people personally as well. Case in point? Mark Goldstein. Mark Goldstein's story appeared on the AARP website in 2020. Mark was laid off from his cybersecurity job in 2017 and has since seen thousands of ads seeking "recent college graduates."[234] "Every bone in your body says, 'Your chances of getting this job are practically zero because they are biased against older employees,'" Goldstein says. "But you try anyway."

---

233 Margaret Kane, Margaret, "Say What? 'Young People are just smarter,'" CNET, March 28, 2007.

234 Kenneth Terrell, "Age Bias That's Barred by Law Appears in Thousands of Job Listings," AARP, October 30, 2019.

It's unclear whether Mark ever connected to a suitable (and wiser) employer, but what is clear is this: words do matter, both in and out of work. Words, when misused, pose a constant risk. They can make the difference between whether a well-qualified person gets a job or not. Too many Marks are out there, suffering from an age bias that we will all be subject to one day unless someone knows how to freeze time.

HOW DOES ARTIFICIAL INTELLIGENCE FIT INTO THE RECRUITING PUZZLE?

Many professions are resistant to change, but they have been slowly adapting to artificial intelligence (AI) in everything from automated document review to recruiting and hiring. These advancements are equally applicable to traditional office settings, remote workforces, and hybrid workforces with both in-person and remote teams.

Diversity AI recruiting is one of the keys to the sustainable success of a company. Artificial intelligence (AI) can recruit, but what good are our AI systems if they inherit its programmers' biases?

Going back to the work of Vivienne Ming, she states a fundamental fact about modern AI: if you do not know how to solve a problem, AI cannot solve the problem for you. In other words, if you hold an implicit bias in your hiring of women or minorities, AI won't magically democratize the process.[235]

---

235 Vivienne Ming, "From Cognitive Modeling to Labor Markets" (EdLab Seminar, Vialogues, April 1, 2015).

Hope, though, still shines through because we can train AI to ignore the things that don't impact a professional's job performance—things like sexual orientation, race, or gender.

Vivienne tells us that AI will reflect our own ethical choices right back at us. So, arguably, AI will make smarter decisions if we make smarter decisions first. By knowing something about the problem we are trying to solve, and by hiring human programmers who have engaged with real-world problems, we can create, train, and refine artificial intelligence systems to be more diverse.

If we understand issues on a more human level and stop auto-prioritizing Joe over Jose, Aiden over Anjali, AI will follow suit. Subsequent inclusion of diverse employees, of course, will still be up to us.

"AI is a phenomenally human technology," Vivienne states, "if we choose to use it that way." In the coming years, the distinction between artificial intelligence and humans will continue to blur. We need to ask ourselves: will we contribute to others' sense of belonging, or will we destroy it?

STEPS TO MORE INCLUSIVE RECRUITING

Creating a diverse and connected work environment starts with inclusive hiring practices. Great candidates can get passed by during the hiring process if we don't protect against biases. Here are some ways to get the best candidates in the door:

START WITH THE JOB LISTING

Bias at work can start before a hiring team even sees a résumé. According to a LinkedIn gender diversity report, women can be deterred from applying to a job they are qualified for based on the job description alone.[236] Many companies unintentionally exhibit strong linguistic bias in recruiting and hiring, using language that hardly sounds inclusive like "recent graduate," "digital native," and "gunner."

Job listings should be neutral and avoid language that might turn off a strong candidate. Tools like Gender Decoder or Textio can help identify controversially worded phrases that come off too masculine or negative.

I took a closer look at Textio's age inclusion guidance, which helps Textio's organizations build more inclusive work environments by raising writers' awareness of the unintended bias that may be excluding people across different age groups.

Textio's age graph shows writers how their job postings may resonate with different age groups: it calls attention to specific language that could be alienating like "21st century skills" or "youthful energy." Using Textio's age inclusion guidance, writers can increase their writing's appeal to *all* job seekers. By optimizing their language across all age demographics, writers will attract a broader and more age-inclusive talent pool.237 These apps also detect biases based on other identifying characteristics, which is a good thing. Some critics, though, make an interesting point: scrubbing job postings of

236 "Language Matters: How Words Impact Men and Women in the Workplace," Linkedin Business, accessed August 9, 2020.

237 "How We Make Textio," Textio, accessed August 8, 2020.

"gendered" words can accidentally make the problem worse by assuming that certain words are more often linked to certain genders. For example, is it fair for software to scrub the word "leader" for seeming like a male word? Isn't that generalization in and of itself biased?

It's an interesting debate, no matter what side you fall on.

ENLIST THE HELP OF ARTIFICIAL INTELLIGENCE

The typical way of assessing applicants before an interview is by having recruiters review résumés. Many studies have shown that this process leads to unconscious bias against minorities, women, and older workers.[238] LinkedIn and other sites have about 250 applicants apply for any open role. Since that means that millions of people are applying for a fraction of those job openings, recruiters usually focus on the 10 percent to 20 percent they think will show the most promise: and those candidates almost always include Ivy League and employee referral candidates, which can reduce the diversity and inclusiveness of the pool.[239]

Artificial Intelligence holds real promise for eliminating bias in hiring because it can minimize unconscious human bias and assess the whole pipeline of candidates. A lot of current AI recruiting tools have flaws, but they can be fixed.[240]

---

238 Corinne A. Moss-Racusin et al., "Science faculty's subtle gender biases favor male students," *Proceedings of the National Academy of Sciences of the United States of America* 109, no. 41(October 2012): 16474-79.

239 Lauren Rivera, "Firms Are Wasting Millions Recruiting on Only a Few Campuses," Harvard Business Review, October 23, 2015.

240 Peter Cappelli, "Your Approach to Hiring Is All Wrong," Harvard Business Review, May 2019.

Open AI and the Future of Life Institute are already working on design principles to make AI more fair and ethical by embracing concepts like the principle of the human value that says that AI systems should be designed and operated "so as to be compatible with ideals of human dignity, rights, freedoms, and cultural diversity."[241]

HireVue is a software application that can use AI (artificial intelligence) to evaluate candidate responses to video interviews. As candidates record themselves responding to interview questions, AI assesses the candidate according to the role's actual performance metrics. This provides a valid, bias-free success indicator.[242] You can then take top scoring candidates to the next stage of your hiring process, having already completed one round of interviews.

AI also has the ability to assess everyone in the pipeline at once instead of having humans pre-select a large number of applicants who are prematurely removed due to time constraints. A real-life example is Airbnb, whose previous recruitment plan actually actively sought to find commonalities between candidates, with the thought being that people could form deeper connections if they shared common ground.[243] AI was able to detect that this was leading to unconscious bias. Airbnb restructured its entire recruiting process and created objective scoresheets, so each candidate

241 "Asilomar AI Principles." Future of Life Institute. Accessed August 9, 2020.

242 Sabel, Jon-Mark, "How AI is Transforming Pre-Hire Assessments [Webinar Recap]," HireVue, August 24, 2017.

243 Frida Polli, "Using AI to Eliminate Bias from Hiring," Harvard Business Review, October 29, 2019.

was evaluated fairly and objectively.[244] As humans, we don't need to, nor should we, artificially shrink the candidate pipeline based on the wrong criteria. Artificial intelligence allows us to use a truly automated top-of-funnel process so we can eliminate the bias.[245]

Some states are already taking action. The California State Assembly is promoting diversity in hiring by passing a resolution to use unbiased hiring technology, and the San Francisco DA is using "blind sentencing" AI in criminal justice proceedings.[246] Is it a perfect system without flaws? Of course not. Room for improvement exists in both human and AI recruiting. The work will never be complete. Like the humans they seek, recruiters will need to constantly pursue new tools, techniques, and practices to flourish. Here are some factors to consider and questions to ask:

- While preparing job listings and recruiting candidates: Are we really willing to do things differently with recruiting? Are we willing to work toward de-biasing behavior when key decisions are made for job postings and résumé screenings? Are we making diverse slates the norm, and have we identified underrepresented groups? Are we using inclusive ads on social media? Are we looking for diverse candidates where they are instead of expecting them to discover us? Have we expanded our internal referral

244 Chiradeep Basu Mallick, "4 Workplace Diversity Trends for 2019," HR Technologist, December 18, 2018.

245 Frida Polli, "Using AI to Eliminate Bias from Hiring," Harvard Business Review, October 29, 2019.

246 Reggie Jones-Sawyer and Julian Canete, "La Opinión: How to End Biased Hiring in California," Fair Hiring California, September 6, 2019.

system to include a broader range of backgrounds? Are we implementing sponsorship programs in underrepresented areas to prepare marginalized groups for future positions?

- During the interview process: Are we resisting the candidate because the person is not what you're "used to" seeing? Are we using lack of "culture fit" as a reason to bypass a well-qualified candidate? Are we looking past résumés to test for cross-cultural competencies?
- After meeting the candidates: Have you assessed any gaps in thinking and planned to implement changes as necessary? Do we need to partner with outside consultants to help us discover and solve any issues?

EXPAND YOUR NETWORK

If you regularly rely on current employee referrals, and your current work environment is pretty homogeneous, your pool of applicants will look pretty homogeneous as well. It's important to share job listings with a diverse group of people. Make efforts to attend networking and community events that center around attracting diverse job seekers.

As we compete for the best and brightest talent, we have to remember to consider people's cultural diversity with different backgrounds, experiences, ideas, and abilities. Set your organization as one committed to diversity and inclusion. Put your money where your mouth is.

Engaging and recruiting people is an important goal, but you can't do that until you find them in the first place. Remote workforces eliminate the problem of limiting searches to local candidates in local areas. Whether your workplace is in person, remote, or hybrid, sourcing and finding people is the most important factor in hiring a diverse employee pool. You can't recruit, message, or network with someone you haven't found. Take the time and do the research to find people where they are—don't always make them come to you, because even if they find you in the vast world of job openings, they may never be seen.

Vivienne Ming says it really well: "Discrimination isn't done by villains. It's done by humans."[247]

---

247 Patel, Bindra Anjali. "Artificial Intelligence: Unleashing Human Potential." *SweaTours: Law Student Well Being. December 2, 2019. Podcast audio, 35:39.*

CHAPTER ELEVEN

HOW TO IMPROVE WELLBEING

———

"Good health IS good business."

- PAUL DRECHSLER, CHAIRMAN/
CEO, WATES GROUP LIMITED[248]

When I joined Thrive Global's *Overcoming Lawyer Burnout* as Editor-at-Large in 2019, I learned about what prompted Founder Arianna Huffington to launch the behavior-changing platform, designed to prevent burnout and enhance wellbeing.

Arianna's wake-up call came when she discovered a pool of blood in her office. The blood was hers. Arianna had been running the *Huffington Post* at the time, and she was so

---

248 Paul Drechsler, "'Good Health IS Good Business.' Obsidian Systems (@ obsidianza). Twitter, April 7, 2020.

exhausted that she passed out near her desk, shattering her cheekbone on her way down.

Looking back, Arianna says the incident was the "best thing that ever happened to me," a wake-up call that led her to sell her news site to AOL for $315 million so she could shift her focus to wellbeing, burnout, and the launch of Thrive Global.[249]

Many of our workplaces' culture dictates a 24/7 cycle, one in which burnout is not just possible—it's inevitable. "This really goes back to the first industrial revolution where we started treating human beings like machines," Arianna says. "The goal of the machine is to minimize downtime, but the human operating system is not a machine. And downtime is not a bug, but a feature of the system."[250]

We have a strong connection between our wellbeing, our sleep, and our productivity. Just ask Jeff Bezos, founder of Amazon and the richest man in the world. He regularly sleeps 8 hours a day because he makes better decisions as a result.[251]

MENTAL, OCCUPATIONAL, AND SOCIAL WELLBEING
We are at an inflection point as companies start realizing the critical value of wellbeing in the workplace. Still, we can't

---

249 "Sleep Deprivation: An Oft-Ignored Occupational Hazard in Health care." Healio News, May 10, 2017.

250 Ibid.

251 Dan Moskowitz, "The 5 Richest People In the World." Investopedia. Last modified, March 30, 2020.

help our employees with their emotional, social, and workplace wellbeing if they don't talk to us about it.

To develop those wellbeing elements, we need to build emotional skills first— skills like positive thinking, vulnerability, and empathy. So how do we do that? It often starts with one courageous voice who is willing to speak openly, vulnerably, and authentically, like Lisa Smith.

Lisa is a recovery advocate, writer, speaker, podcast host, lawyer, and author of *Girl Walks Out of a Bar*. Through her talks, book, podcast, and uncanny ability to listen, she helps others by sharing her personal experiences with depression, addiction, and recovery. In her book, she shares memories that are both raw and relatable:

> *"My slide into round-the-clock drinking was something I was entitled to. It made me ashamed, and it made me despise myself, but it also made me feel better because it was a crucial weapon in the fight against being me. I felt entitled to do whatever it took to win the battle against the unfair circumstances of my life, this life in which I played by all the right rules and still ended up miserable and lonely and riddled with self-hatred."*[252]

Lisa's story is compelling to all of us, regardless of whether we have personally stared down alcoholism or not. Her book recounts her descent into and recovery from "high-functioning" alcohol and cocaine addictions in a prominent New

---

252 Lisa Smith, *Girl Walks Out of a Bar: A Memoir* (New York: Select Books, 2016), 150.

York City law firm. Her story launched her to the forefront of the movement to advance wellbeing in the legal profession. She now talks openly about her struggles, hoping that her honesty will encourage others to show empathy, talk openly, and listen compassionately.

I interviewed Lisa for the *Sweatours* wellbeing podcast in 2019, where Lisa aptly described the nature of addiction and its often connected self-loathing: "It's non-discriminatory," she told me. "No age, gender, race, or status is immune." She also talked about how addiction ties into the corporate culture and the increased push for support programs and open communication in the workplace. Education on depression and addiction can chip away at the stigma behind these issues and make it okay to want to talk about it.[253]

Let's face it: whether we struggle with substance abuse or not, we are all addicted to something. We all have our demons. People like Lisa open up their worlds to us and teach us how to love ourselves, not merely despite, but *because of* our struggles.

HOW TO IMPROVE MENTAL, EMOTIONAL, AND WORKPLACE WELLBEING—THE NON-MEASURABLES:

- Communicate openly between departments and make it a priority. Have honest chats and make sure all team members have a say, and that they're valued team members.

---

253 Anjali Bindra Patel, "Lisa Smith: From Breaking Down to Breaking Through," December 9, 2019, in *SweaTours: Law Student Well Being*, podcast audio, 26:00.

Follow-through on your promises. If things go wrong, apologize.

- Make a point to discuss mental, emotional, and workplace wellbeing. Start by having a discussion around the comment we often hear after we tragically lose someone to suicide: "But she didn't look like she was depressed..." What is a depressed person supposed to look like? Educate your workforce on the reality that depression is not a "one size fits all" look. Some people may have low energy, while others are highly energetic. Some may overeat, while others don't eat at all. Get a checklist on other signs and symptoms of mental health challenges and have an open communication channel.[254]

- Make it clear that employees can count on management, that you can be trusted, and that you, in turn, trust them. One way to show trust is to let team members do their work without micromanaging.[255]

- Embrace NOT being an expert. Sometimes just listening compassionately can go a long way. Google is an excellent example of this (more on this in a minute).

- Take the time to recharge. Take a break so you can sustain yourself for the long haul. Advocating for diversity and inclusion as a way to improve wellbeing is not a sprint—it's a marathon. Take the time to take care of yourself and remember that our efforts to improve wellbeing are more than today's battle; it's tomorrow's movement as well.

Google initiated the "Blue Dot" program, which is like peer to peer counseling, but without the credentialing, since no

254 "Depression Symptom Checklist," Trintellix, accessed August 9, 2020.
255 Holly Henderson Brower et al., "Want Your Employees to Trust You? Show You Trust Them," Harvard Business Review, July 5, 2017.

one is officially coaching or counseling anyone. Instead, they are certified listeners who listen with an open and compassionate mind, an endangered art form. Listeners are around for colleagues who need an ear. A blue dot sticker identifies listeners on their name tag or laptop. Imagine an army of Brian Cubans with blue stickers that convey the message, "I'm here for you." It's that simple.

The Blue Dot program, at last count, has over 400 listeners, who all watched a 30-minute video about how to get started as compassionate listeners. The steps behind compassionate listening at work seem simple enough—paraphrasing and avoiding judgment and opinions, for example—but it's not easy, whether at Google or within your workplaces. The fact is that we are usually paid to give our opinions, whether in currency or through validation of getting "likes" on social media.[256]

Again, the underlying message of Blue Dot is about forming a sense of community to assuage the pent-up anxiety, stress, and depression that between 18-30 percent of people say disrupts their work.[257] Knowing that there's a group of people to say "I'm here for you" can help add a layer of psychological safety to our lives that so many of us crave.

Programs like Blue Dot are meant to be a low-barrier way to relieve some of the common anxiety in workforces everywhere. Just because it's not measured doesn't mean it doesn't work.

---

256 Lila MacLellan, "Google is Running an Employee Mental Health Project Without any Metrics," Quartz at Work, June 25, 2019.

257 Lila MacLellan, "Millennials Experience Work-Disrupting Anxiety at Twice the US average Rate," Quartz at Work, December 5, 2018.

PHYSICAL AND FINANCIAL WELLBEING: THE MEASURABLES

To develop our physical and financial wellbeing, metrics help implement effective strategies in our daily lives. This is where workplace wellbeing programs have shown their strengths.

Wellbeing programs do more than promote healthy habits. They are a way of showing employees that you care. According to the 2018 Global Talent Trends Study, half of all employees want to see a stronger focus on their company's wellbeing. This includes an emphasis on physical and financial wellness.[258]

HOW TO IMPROVE PHYSICAL AND FINANCIAL WELLBEING—THE MEASURABLES:

- A workplace wellness program customized with various wellness initiatives like on-site health screenings, wellness challenges, and regular lunch-and-learns for financial planning and savings are examples of wellness initiatives that can be implemented year-round.
- Employers should offer employees opportunities for stress relief and opportunities for physical activity. Investing in standing desks, meditation apps, or fitness classes are ways that employers can impact employee wellbeing. Look into personal trainers in your local area who can help with exercise programs, as well as motivational coaching.

---

258 Robyn Whalen, "The Role of Financial Health in Employee Wellbeing," Total Wellness, August 7, 2017.

- Invest in financial planning training that includes budgeting for monthly bills, emergency savings, reducing debt, basics on investing, and retirement planning. The Consumer Financial Protection Bureau offers free resources, and specialists such as JJ. Wenrich, author of *Teaching Kids to Buy Stocks,* do on-site training for businesses.

WELLBEING: CREATING BETTER WORKSPACES FOR ON-SITE EMPLOYEES

Cubicles. Co-working spaces. Couches. Beanbags. Standing desks. Angular desks. Ergonomic chairs. Exercise ball chairs. If it's an existing workplace product, someone has tested it out.

How do we know whether any of these approaches are effective? The answer: it depends on what you need. Is it increased physical wellbeing? More collaboration and social connection?

Silicon Valley has been studying the tight correlation between personal interactions,

performance, and wellbeing for a while now. Companies like Samsung have created massive outdoor spaces where they hope engineers and salespeople will mingle, collaborate, and connect.[259]

Here are a few ways companies are designing optimal wellbeing spaces:

---

259 Ben Waber et al., "Workplaces That Move People," Harvard Business Review, October 2014.

- Design offices to reflect on how 21st century digital work happens.

The tools we use to get work done have changed a lot more than the buildings we work in. Many of us are working remotely at least part of the time, and when we do come in, it's so we can brainstorm with other people. In a situation like this, open-concept spaces allow for increased probability of interactions that lead to innovation and productivity, enhancing a person's overall sense of purpose and wellbeing.

- Strategic Coffee Machines.

In Alex "Sandy" Pentland's April 2012 HBR article, "The New Science of Building Great Teams," Pentland deployed badges that tracked how people interacted and spent time. (Devices were worn on an opt-in basis, and individual data was anonymous and unavailable to employers.) Pentland figured out three successful means of communication:

- *exploration* (interacting with people in many other social groups)
- *engagement* (interacting with people within your social group, in equal doses) and
- *energy* (interacting with more people overall)[260]

Spaces designed to promote these activities increased the likelihood of collisions—and the data repeatedly demonstrated that more collisions create positive outcomes. Companies took note and made changes like replacing the mini coffee makers with more extensive, more pleasant, consolidated

---

260 Alex Pentland, "The New Science of Building Great Teams," Harvard Business Review, April 2012.

coffee machines where people who may not otherwise interact would engage with one another in an informal setting.

Each company needs to figure out their goals before deciding what to put into play—revolving desks, larger common areas, more private areas, or a little bit of each. Talk to your people. What do they need? Small changes to where we work will lead to more significant changes in how we work and enhance our wellbeing on multiple fronts.

WELLBEING: THE DISTRIBUTED WORKFORCE

One factor complicates all the work that companies have been doing to re-imagine their collective workspaces: office buildings are no longer the sole locations for knowledge work. Research from the consulting group Emergent Research suggests that two-thirds of work often happens outside the office.[261]

Remote work and distributed workforces are here to stay, so even the best-designed office spaces need to account for the large number of remote workers who will need their wellbeing addressed in other ways. Over 82 percent of industry leaders state they will allow remote work some, or even most, of the time.[262] Like it or not, we all need to adjust to the "next normal" of remote work. Smart leaders need to figure out how they can best help their employees work productively for

261 "Trends and Insights on the Small Business Economy," Emergent Research, accessed August 9, 2020.

262 Gartner, Inc. "Gartner Survey Reveals 82% of Company Leaders Plan to Allow Employees to Work Remotely Some of the Time." Gartner. July 14, 2020.

the long haul while also taking care of their wellbeing. New norms and behaviors have to be implemented and adjusted to accompany the unique aspects of remote work.

Newly remote teams might be struggling to figure out when to start and stop work, and when to work collaboratively versus when to work alone. One idea to address this issue is to create a shared rhythm for your team. An example of a shared rhythm would be a daily "stand up" at a specific time (a quick chat about what you're up to, and where you need advice) or "quiet zone" hours each day where no one plans meetings or expects responses to their messages. Quiet zones allow for deep concentration on complex projects and enable people to work efficiently and productively, so they do not burn the midnight oil every night.

HOW TO IMPROVE WELLBEING WITH REMOTE WORKERS:

- Encourage breaks. It can be challenging for remote workers to take breaks when work and home environments blend. Assign realistic timelines and achievable goals for remote staff. As an antidote to the "always on" mode of remote work, you can encourage employees to use the time to unplug and relax.[263]
- Provide access to mental health services. The stigma around mental health issues in the US remains. Many people suffering from these symptoms hesitate to talk about those issues in the way they would talk about a physical ailment, like a broken bone. One solution is

---

263 Sasha Butkovich, "Ways to Improve Your Mental Health on Your Lunch Break," Justworks, April 30, 2020.

to offer remote employees access to anonymous mental health services and support that they can access anytime.

- Invest in better remote equipment for your team members: ergonomic chairs, noise-canceling headphones, microphones, etc.
- Communicate like Goldilocks, not too little and not too much. Brene Brown states, "A deep sense of love and belonging is an irreducible need of all people. We are biologically, cognitively, physically, and spiritually wired to love, to be loved, and to belong. When those needs are not met, we don't function as we are meant to. We break. We fall apart. We numb. We ache. We hurt others. We get sick."[264] In a distributed workforce, communication is vital. Too much contact leads to a higher risk of burnout, but too little contact could lead to isolation and lack of engagement.
- Employers should look at the quality of the work, not the amount someone has logged online. Jason Fried, CEO of remote company Basecamp, tells his team members that working overtime is not the way to his heart. In fact, he credits Basecamp's 32-40 hour workweek as the key to its healthy company culture.[265]
- Get a good coach. Using positive psychology and mindfulness concepts, experts like Elina Teboul, who runs The LightUp Lab, help you cultivate and implement the tools

---

264 Brené Brown, *The Gifts of Imperfection: Let Go of Who You Think You're Supposed to Be and Embrace Who You Are* (Center City: Hazelden Publishing, 2010),26.

265 Courtney Connley, "Why the CEO of Basecamp Only Allows Employees to Work 32 Hours a Week." CNBC. Last modified August 4, 2017.

you need to reach your full potential while still maintaining work/life integration.[266]

If you're an employer, understand that employees who have the resources to manage their mental health and wellbeing will be more significant assets to your business.

If you're an employee? Keep in mind: it takes time and effort to build any new skill set—that includes wellbeing skills. Set up a realistic plan, try to stick it to it, lean on others when you need support, and let them lean right back. Care about other people and let them care about you.

---

266 Elina Teboul, "The Light Up Lab," accessed July 3, 2020.

CONCLUSION: WHERE DO WE GO FROM HERE?

———

"Our lives begin to end the day we become silent about things that matter."

- PARAPHRASED FROM MARTIN LUTHER KING, JR.[267]

In their book *Conscious Capitalism*, John Mackey and Raj Sisodia talk about doing what is right *because* it's right. Conscious businesses, they say, have a simple but powerful belief: the right actions undertaken for the right reasons generally lead to good outcomes over time. They treat their stakeholders well because it is the right, humane, and sensible thing to do and because humanity is also smart business practice.

The authors take this analysis a step further by asking, "How would I feel if what I'm doing right now is written up on

———

267 Hanna Hutyra, "123 of the Most Inspiring Martia Luther King Jr. Quotes," Accessed June 1, 2020.

the front page of the *New York Times* or the *Wall Street Journal*?"[268]

Honestly, it's a solid question to ask. If you looked at your company's diversity numbers, what would you see? Would your organization's diversity be broader than gender and race? Would it also be diverse in age, thought, and physical abilities? Would you see the same diversity in the leadership ranks as you saw at the entry-level? What would your workforce say about inclusion and wellbeing? Knowing that almost 7 out of 10 people feel disengaged at work, did you ask your own people how they were and what they needed?

If you took a collective pulse of your organization today, how would your headline read? Would you be proud?

Talking about diversity, inclusion, and wellbeing can be challenging, and initiating company-wide changes to create a more welcoming environment can seem nearly impossible. Companies generally hire through their networks that reflect the race, gender, and ethnicity of the people in their leadership ranks. But as more and more companies move to a remote or distributed workforce, it's time to start asking: does this old school network rule apply anymore?

IMPACTS ON A REMOTE/DISTRIBUTED WORKFORCE

In an increasingly remote workforce, we are no longer confined to searching for the best people in the radius closest to

---

268 John Mackey and Rajendra Sisodia, *Conscious Capitalism: Liberating the Heroic Spirit of Business* (Boston: Harvard Business Review Press, 2013), 209.

our company. We can, and should, search for the best people, period. Those people will be from varying backgrounds, ages, abilities, races, and cultures. Systems can be put in place to make collaboration, creativity, and communication part of the organization's DNA. All of this doesn't happen on its own, though. It happens by choice.

A perfect example of diversity, inclusion, and wellbeing in a remote setting is Kevin Smith from Abstract, a remote start-up discussed throughout the book. Abstract allows its employees to work anywhere in the US because the company believes that creating and nurturing a distributed culture is the key to inclusion. Remote work isn't an adjustment or an afterthought: it's the foundation of how they work.

Co-founders Kevin and Josh (yes, I know the names sound monolithic but hear me out) made it their mission to invest in finding talent from underrepresented communities. They didn't stop at diverse hiring, though. They worked to build cultures that support their employees as multi-hyphenated individuals. Inclusion made their company more resilient by increasing its diverse inputs and perspectives, letting them create better products. It's also the right thing to do.

The founders of Abstract said it best: "How you build is just as important as what you build. Perhaps more so."[269]

---

269 Josh Brewer, Josh, "Inclusion is a Choice," Abstract, January 17, 2019.

CHECKLISTS TO CREATE A BETTER PLACE TO WORK

Regardless of whether your organization embraces remote work, tolerates it, or is unable to implement it, the basic principles of diversity, inclusion, and wellbeing are key to any organization aiming to build a compassionate culture.

When talking about diversity, we often jump to gender and/or race. But diversity is wider than that. It can also be characterized by age, disabilities, diversity in thought, and so much more.

When looking to improve diversity, ask yourself the following:

- Do we have advocates and policies in place for recruiting and hiring of underrepresented groups? Are we meeting our goals? If not, why? If so, how can we improve even further?
- What are you doing to engage with underrepresented communities?
- Have we kept track of retention rates? Who's staying, and why? Who's leaving, and why?
- Does leadership talk regularly about the importance of diversity? Are its actions backing up its words?

Once we have diversity in place, we have to make sure our people can bring their authentic selves to work. When we feel like we won't be accepted or included, we either run and become isolated or mask and become suffocated in our inability to be our authentic selves.

For inclusion and belonging, ask yourself the following:

- Does your culture invite compassionate listening? Do people talk to each other about issues besides work?
- Do you celebrate differences of others, or merely tolerate them?
- Do you encourage people to express new ideas?
- Do you allow open discussions of both successes and failures?
- Do you recognize bias and call it out when you see it? Going against the expectations of the group or polite company isn't easy. Protesting at a march comes with validation of everyone around you but calling out an inappropriate action or statement and going against the tide of the group at work takes a different type of courage. Calling out bias is important in private spaces, not just public ones.
- What do your sexual harassment and workplace policies look like? If you have NDAs, has your legal team addressed its scope? Have you consulted with organizations like the Purple Campaign about ending harassment in the workplace?

Wellbeing is very much connected to diversity and inclusion, even though it is often addressed as some elusive standalone topic to be addressed by a local trainer or physician. To build a compassionate culture, wellbeing of our people has to be addressed. Best-practice diversity and inclusion programs recognize wellbeing as a diversity and inclusion issue. A lot of individuals will experience mental health challenges that may prevent them from participating fully at work. Inclusive employers take a close look at the work environment and practices to identify psychological injury risks and transfer skills to employees for managing stress.

For wellbeing of your workforce, ask yourself the following:

- Are you setting realistic timelines and achievable goals, or are you leading your best team members down a path toward burnout?
- Do you encourage breaks, both mental and physical?
- Do you provide access to mental health services? What are you doing to reduce the stigma of those seeking assistance with mental health?
- Have you addressed the largest sources of stress at your organization? Are they based on financial, social, mental, or physical challenges?
- Do you offer customizable wellbeing programs focused on occupational, physical, financial, emotional, and spiritual wellbeing?

FINAL THOUGHTS

Many companies have started taking steps in the right direction, but our work is far from done. Building inclusive and empathetic communities is an ongoing process and will ultimately distinguish the most successful, enduring organizations from others.

While we may not have all the answers, we know the path forward requires compassionate and empathetic conversations with each other. We have to make the conscious decision to value diversity, inclusion, and wellbeing, and we need to live our missions. We need to honor our differences. We need to celebrate them. We need to embrace them because that is what the successful, compassionate cultures of tomorrow will do.

Looking to our future, it's possible to be both realistic and optimistic at the same time. Many of the challenges we face in the workforce are symptomatic of a larger problem present throughout all of our neighborhoods, schools, and communities.

As a case in point, early in 2020, my son's middle school principal and I met to discuss the huge increase in hate speech at the school. Kids targeted disabled students and minority students and had been saying some truly reprehensible things. The meeting shocked my conscience and shattered my naïve belief that our kids were somehow immune from such hate during the confines of the school day.

I was desperate to help the principal, so I reached out to a reputable connection I had. This connection was a mentor to me, and I knew he had a really good heart.

He empathized and seemed truly sympathetic about the kids on the receiving end of the hate speech. But he was living in another state, so he advised me to reach out to someone local. He said he was too far removed from the situation.

I didn't question his response, but looking back, I really wish I had responded differently to the "too far removed" comment. The *location* of the hate speech, or the unlawful arrest, or the discriminatory hiring and firing is never the point. The *inequality* is the point. The resulting *complacency* is the point.

Racism, inequality, and exclusion are eerily similar to the coronavirus of 2020. It's not "too far removed" from anyone, because it's everywhere. We might not see it, but that doesn't mean it isn't there: it's in our communities, it's in our work-places, it's in our social circles, and it's in our families. Like a virus, it can spread asymptomatically— some people might not even be aware that their beliefs and actions at work are harming others.

After George Floyd's horrific murder in 2020, our "too far removed" sentiment changed overnight. Anti-racism pro-tests ramped up across the United States. We talked about equality. We marched about equality. We read about equality. We educated others on what we learned about equality. We posted on social media about equality. We saw Hollywood A-listers making PSA announcements about equality. It was impressive.

But here's what I learned after my protesting: it wasn't enough.

Here's what I learned after posting on Twitter and arguing about equality on LinkedIn: it wasn't enough.

Here's what I learned after reading, posting, researching, teaching, and writing a book about equality: it wasn't enough.

Reading about diversity, inclusion, and wellbeing is great. Publicly stating our commitment to building compassionate cultures at work is laudable. But this book, or hundreds of others, can't change your culture. Only people can do that. Only action can do that.

When it comes to treating people inclusively and compassion-ately at work, often our first instinct is to educate ourselves, and this is admittedly a pretty critical piece of the puzzle. But we're not done once we've immersed ourselves in the stats, research, strategies, and the metrics.

I learned that being "woke" isn't just about saying the right thing. It's about doing it. Are our actions in line with our social media posts pushing for equality?

To truly build a compassionate culture, we can't just educate ourselves and leave the rest to chance. We need to connect. We need to listen, we need to ask questions, and we need to assert our own rights to be heard when our voices are lost.

As leaders, we need to ask why someone under our watch would feel unheard in the first place, and we need to fix that by improving our inclusion policies, exercising compassion, prioritizing wellbeing, and forming channels for our people to connect, listen, lean in and advocate for what's right.

The books we read will give us guidance. The speakers we hear will give us hope. The compassionate connections we form will lead to impact.

There isn't a single right way to move forward. We may be unsure about how to have tough conversations. Some people may fear that, as a majority group, they lack the legitimacy to have an opinion. They have the responsibility to push past those fears, and we all have the responsibility to let them in. We need to create a safe environment for discussion and be honest that no one person in the workplace will have all the answers, but that a united group can improve together over time.

We may struggle along the way. We may miscalculate at times and divide ourselves further. We may have to recalibrate and try again. But if we remain resilient and move forward in solidarity, we *will* create the change we need to see in the workplace and in ourselves.

ACKNOWLEDGEMENTS

———

I want to thank my husband, who carried the load for both of us as I spent the past few months repeatedly complaining about how I could no longer differentiate between commas and periods unless we were in a brightly-lit room. "Wow, I think this is the first time I'm hearing about this," he calmly told me every evening for seven months. Thank you for being there, babe.

I also want to thank both of my parents, who supported me through this journey and shared their own insights about their lives as an "other." To Daddy: when you shared your stories and walked me through your decades of professional journeys, I got to know you in a whole new way. Thank you for being my cheerleader and my friend.

A special thank you to all the innovators, leaders, and change agents who inspired me to write this book, and to the people who agreed to be part of it.

I also want to thank the man who messaged me to say, "It's cool you're writing a book, but I probably won't read the whole thing." Thanks for being honest and keeping me humble, I think.

To Rebecca and Cassandra, my editors, thank you for being my fiercest supporters when I needed it most. To Eric and Brian, thank you for leading the charge.

To all the companies, institutions, law firms, and individuals who pre-ordered this book, I can't thank you enough. To RPB Consulting, DCA, and local schools who believed in this book, thank you for your faith in my ability to use my voice. Also, a special thanks to Kim, Julie, and Jones Walker for believing in this book and in me. And to the #PeloLawMoms who have been there for me through this process: thank you.

Finally, I want to acknowledge our amazing kids: Aarav, Saranya, and Ishaana, who have been my partners in crime during this year of quarantine. Without you, this book probably would have been completed a long time ago. Still, I want you to know something: mediating daily arguments over stale Oreos, missing laptop chargers, and dog walking duties is part and parcel of the best job I will ever have, alongside the best humans I will ever know. I wouldn't change a thing about you. I love you to the moon and beyond.

If you have enjoyed reading this book (or even if you haven't), please consider leaving a review on Amazon, Goodreads, or wherever you hang out online, so you can help other people decide if they should read it. You can learn more about diversity, inclusion, and wellbeing at www.sweatours.com or email me at anjali@sweatours.com. I am always down for an engaging conversation.

APPENDIX

———

INTRODUCTION

Frey, William H. "Diversity Defines the Millennial Generation." Brookings. June 28, 2016. https://www.brookings.edu/blog/the-avenue/2016/06/28/diversity-defines-the-millennial-generation/.

Frey, William H. "The US will become 'Minority White' in 2045, Census Projects." Brookings. March 14, 2018. https://www.brookings.edu/blog/the-avenue/2018/03/14/the-us-will-become-minority-white-in-2045-census-projects/.

CHAPTER 1: WHAT IS DIVERSITY?

Appelbaum, Lauren. "Cast of Hollywood Changemakers Fight Stigmas During Americans with Disabilities Act Celebration." Respectability. July 24, 2020. https://www.respectability.org/2020/07/hollywood-ada30/.

Appelbaum, Lauren. "Netflix's Newest Series Takes Disability Inclusion to a New Level," Respectability, January 13, 2020, https://www.respectability.org/2020/01/netflix-healing-pow-ers-of-dude/.

Bersin, Josh, and Tomas Chamorro-Premuzic. "The Case for Hiring Older Workers." Harvard Business Review. September 26, 2019. https://hbr.org/2019/09/the-case-for-hiring-older-workers.

Big Demands and High Expectations: The Deloitte Millennial Survey," Deloitte, January 2014, https://www2.deloitte.com/content/dam/Deloitte/global/Documents/About-Deloitte/gx-dttl-2014-millennial-survey-report.pdf.

Bindon, David, Simone Askew, Joy Schaeffer, Tony Smith, Care Kehn, Jack Lowe, Netteange Monaus, Ashley Salgado, and Maria Blom. Policy Proposal: An Anti-Racist West Point. June 25, 2020. Slideshow. https://www.slideshare.net/TimothyBerry8/an-anti-racist-west-point.

Bolden-Barrett, Valerie. "Gen Z Seeks cognitive diversity at work." HR Dive, February 25, 2020, https://www.hrdive.com/news/generation-z-wants-cognitive-diversity-at-work/572704/.

Calfas, Jennifer. "CDC: 1 in 5 American Adults Live with a Disability." Mississippi Department of Rehabilitation Services. July 31, 2015. https://www.mdrs.ms.gov/Pages/American-adults-living-with-disability.aspx.

Cohn, Emily. "Here Are All the Openly Gay CEOs In The Fortune 500." HuffPost. October 30, 2014. https://www.huffpost.com/entry/gay-ceos-fortune-500_n_6074768.

Dolan, Kevin, Vivian Hunt, Sara Prince, and Sandra Sancier-Sultan. "Diversity During COVID-19 Still Matters." McKinsey & Company. May 19, 2020. https://www.mckinsey.com/featured-insights/diversity-and-inclusion/diversity-still-matters.

Estrada, Sheryl. "Diversity, culture not top strategic priority for most leaders." HR Dive. March 4, 2020. https://www.hrdive.com/news/diversity-culture-not-top-strategic-priority-for-most-leaders/573474/.

Fry, Richard. "Millennials are the largest generation in the US labor force." Pew Research Center. April 11, 2018. https://www.pewresearch.org/fact-tank/2018/04/11/millennials-largest-generation-us-labor-force/.

Littenberg-Weisberg, Sam, and Erica Spates, creators. The Healing Power of Dude. January 13, 2020. https://www.netflix.com/title/80239306.

"Malcolm Forbes Quotes." Brainy Quote. Accessed September 5, 2020. https://www.brainyquote.com/quotes/malcolm_forbes_151513.

"Mental Illness, including Anxiety, Bipolar Disorder, Depression and More." Respectability. Accessed July 30, 2020. https://www.respectability.org/inclusion-toolkits/mental-illness/.

Merriam-Webster. s.v. "Race(n.)." Accessed July 27,2020. https://www.merriam-webster.com/dictionary/determinant.

"Occupation By Sex And Median Earnings In The Past 12 Months (in 2018 Inflation-Adjusted Dollars) For The Full-Time, Year-

Round Civilian Employed Population 16 Years And Over."
United States Census Bureau. 2018. https://data.census.gov/
cedsci/table?q=s2412&hidePreview=true&tid=ACSST1Y2018.
S2412&vintage=2018&g=0100000US.04000.001.

Palmer, Kimberly. "10 Things You Should Know About Age Discrimination." AARP. February 20, 2017. https://www.aarp.org/
work/on-the-job/info-2017/age-discrimination-facts.html.

Parikh, Nish. "Diversity and Inclusion Matters To The Workforce Of The Future." Forbes. May 9, 2018. https://www.
forbes.com/sites/forbeshumanresourcescouncil/2018/05/09/
diversity-and-inclusion-matters-to-the-workforce-of-the-fu-
ture/#27758a58771b.

Parker, Chris, Anita Ricketts, Niraj Kataria, and Hundley Lissiah
Taylor.

Saska, Sarah. "How to Define Diversity, Equity, and Inclusion at
Work,' Accessed Aug 1, 2020. https://www.cultureamp.com/
blog/how-to-define-diversity-equity-and-inclusion-at-work/.

Schwantes, Marcel. "A New Study Reveals 70 Percent of Workers
Say They are Actively Looking for a New Job." Inc. December 4,
2018. https://www.inc.com/marcel-schwantes/a-new-study-re-
veals-70-percent-of-workers-say-they-are-actively-looking-for-
a-new-job-heres-reason-in-5-words.html.

Soares, Rachel, and Liz Mulligan-Ferry. "Report: 2013 Catalyst
Census: Fortune 500 Women Board Directors." Catalyst.
December 10, 2016. https://www.catalyst.org/research/2013-cat-
alyst-census-fortune-500-women-board-directors/.

Stoll, John D. "For CEOs, Pressure Is On to Pivot From 'Say' to 'Do' on Inequality." The Wall Street Journal. June 26, 2020. https://www.wsj.com/articles/for-ceos-pressure-is-on-to-pivot-from-say-to-do-on-inequality-11593183622.

Storer, Christopher, dir. Hasan Minhaj: Homecoming King. 2017; Davis, CA: Netflix.

Sweet, Julie, and Ellyn Shook. "Getting to Equal 2020: The Hidden Value of Culture Makers." Accenture, 2020. https://www.accenture.com/us-en/about/inclusion-diversity/culture-equality-research.

"The Nielsen Total Audience Report: Q1 2017." Nielsen. July 12, 2017. https://www.nielsen.com/us/en/insights/report/2017/the-nielsen-total-audience-report-q1-2017/.

"Where's the Diversity in Fortune 500 CEOs?" DiversityInc. October 8, 2012. https://www.diversityinc.com/wheres-the-diversity-in-fortune-500-ceos/.

CHAPTER 2: WHAT IS INCLUSION?

Baldoni, John. "Fostering The Sense of Belonging Promotes Success." Forbes. January 22, 2017. https://www.forbes.com/sites/johnbaldoni/2017/01/22/fostering-the-sense-of-belonging-promotes-success/#16b535d110f2.

Bhuiyan, Johana, Sam Dean, and Suhauna Hussain. "Black and brown tech workers share their experiences of racism on the job." Los Angeles Times. June 24, 2020. https://www.latimes.

com/business/technology/story/2020-06-24/diversity-in-tech-tech-workers-tell-their-story.

Bleiweis, Robin, "Quick Facts About the Gender Wage Gap," American Progress, March 24, 2020, https://www.american-progress.org/issues/women/reports/2020/03/24/482141/quick-facts-gender-wage-gap/.

Carr, Evan W., Andrew Reece, Gabriella Rosen Kellerman, and Alexi Robichaux. "The Value of Belonging at Work." Harvard Business Review. December 16, 2019. https://hbr.org/2019/12/the-value-of-belonging-at-work.

Coffman, Julie, and Bill Neuenfeldt. "Everyday Moments of Truth: Frontline Managers Are Key to Women's Career Aspirations." Bain & Company. June 17, 2014. https://www.bain.com/insights/everyday-moments-of-truth/.

Danilova, Maria, "Study shows gender bias at an early age," Boston Globe, January 26, 2017, https://www.bostonglobe.com/news/nation/2017/01/26/study-shows-gender-bias-early-age/QqkTTbd2CYFR7TGAGjBLZL/story.html.

"Diversity & Inclusion." SHRM-LI. Accessed July 28, 2020. http://shrmli.org/community/diversity-inclusion/.

Haley, Nikki R. With All Due Respect: Defending America with Grit and Grace. New York: St. Martin's Press, 2019.

Jacobi, Tonja, and Dylan Schweers. "Female Supreme Court Justices Are Interrupted More by Male Justices and Advocates." Harvard Business Review. April 11, 2017. https://hbr.

org/2017/04/female-supreme-court-justices-are-interrupted-more-by-male-justices-and-advocates.

Kirkland, Rik, and Iris Bohnet. "Focusing on what works for workplace diversity." McKinsey & Company. April 7, 2017. https://www.mckinsey.com/featured-insights/gender-equality/focusing-on-what-works-for-workplace-diversity#.

Lieberman, Matthew, and Naomi Eisenberger. "The Pains and pleasures of social life: a social cognitive neuroscience approach." Science 323, no. 5916 (2009): 890-891. https://doi.org/10.1126/science.1170008.

Lipman, Joanne. That's What She Said: What Men Need to Know (and Women Need to Tell Them) About Working Together. New York: William Morrow, 2018.

Murthy, Vivek H. Together: The Healing Power of Human Connection in a Sometimes Lonely World. New York: Harper Wave, 2020.

O'Hara, Robert, "Artist Interview with Rovert O'Hara interview." By Tim Sanford. Playwrights Horizons. accessed November 10, 2014. https://www.playwrightshorizons.org/shows/trailers/artist-interview-robert-ohara/.

Riley, Andrew. "Ostracism more damaging than bullying in the workplace." The University of British Columbia. May 29, 2014. https://news.ubc.ca/2014/05/29/better-to-be-bullied-than-ignored-in-the-workplace-study/

Rivera, Lauren A. "Guess Who Doesn't Fit In at Work." The New York Times. May 30, 2015. https://www.nytimes.com/2015/05/31/opinion/sunday/guess-who-doesnt-fit-in-at-work.html.

Robbins, Mike. Bring Your Whole Self to Work: How Vulnerability Unlocks Creativity, Connection, and Performance. Carlsbad: Hay House, 2018.

Rohe, William M., and Mark Lindblad. "Reexaming the Social Benefits of Homeownership after the Housing Crisis." Paper presented at Homeownership Built to Last: Lessons from the Housing Crisis on Sustaining Homeownership for Low-Income and Minority Families, April 1 and 2, 2013. Boston, MA. https://www.jchs.harvard.edu/sites/default/files/hbtl-04.pdf.

Serafeim, George. "Corporate Resilience and Response During COVID-19." State Street. April 2020. https://www.statestreet.com/ideas/articles/ssa-corporate-resiliency.html.

Sherbin, Laura, and Ripa Rashid. "Diversity Doesn't Stick Without Inclusion." Harvard Business Review. February 1, 2017. https://hbr.org/2017/02/diversity-doesnt-stick-without-inclusion.

Silva, Laura (Laura Silva). "To the companies, I am not applauding your #blacklivesmatter post." Linkedin, June 2020.

Smith, Kevin. "Why remote work is inclusion work." Abstract. July 10, 2019. https://www.abstract.com/blog/remote-work-inclusion.

"The State of the Gender Pay Gap in 2020." Payscale. Accessed September 5, 2020. https://www.payscale.com/data/gender-pay-gap.

Twaronite, Karyn. "The Surprising Power of Simply Asking Coworkers How They're Doing." Harvard Business Review. February 28, 2019. https://hbr.org/2019/02/the-surprising-power-of-simply-asking-coworkers-how-theyre-doing.

CHAPTER 3 WHAT IS WELLBEING?

Bateman, Kristen. "How I get It Done: Sara Blakely of Spanx." The Cut. June 26, 2018. https://www.thecut.com/2018/06/how-i-get-it-done-sara-blakely-of-spanx.html.

Brand, Sarah L., Jo Thompson Coon, Lora E. Fleming, Lauren S. Carroll, Alison Bethel, and Katrina Wyatt. "Whole-system approaches to improving the health and wellbeing of healthcare workers: A systematic review." PLoS One 12, no. 12 (December 2017). https://doi.org/10.1371/journal.pone.0188418

Briody, Blaire. "Sara Blakely: Start Small, Think Big, Scale Fast." Stanford Graduate School of Business. June 21, 2018. https://www.gsb.stanford.edu/insights/sara-blakely-start-small-think-big-scale-fast.

Buchanan, Bree, and James C. Coyle, Anne Brafford, Josh Camson, Charles Gruber, Terry Harrell, David B. Jaffe, Tracy L. Kepler, Patrick Krill, et al. "The Path to Lawyer Well-being." American Bar. August 14, 2017. https://www.americanbar.org/content/dam/aba/images/abanews/ThePathToLawyerWellBeingReportRevFINAL.pdf.

Field, Hayden. "What It's Like Inside Spanx Headquarters." Entrepreneur. November 15, 2019. https://www.entrepreneur.com/article/341841.

Field, Hayden. "What It's Like Inside Spanx Headquarters." Entrepreneur. November 15, 2019. https://www.entrepreneur.com/article/341841.

Goleman, Daniel. Destructive Emotions: A Scientific Dialogue with the Dalai Lama. New York: Bantam Books, 2003.

https://assets.entrepreneur.com/images/misc/1572972651_ent19_dec_officespace-spanx2.jpg.

Instagram, 2019 Spanx Page Stories.

Keeman, Alexis, Katharina Näswall, Sanna Malinen, and Joana Kuntz. "Employee Wellbeing: Evaluating a Wellbeing Intervention in Two Settings." Frontiers in Psychology 8 (April 2017). https://doi.org/10.3389/fpsyg.2017.00505.

Lieberman, Matthew, and Naomi Eisenberger. "The Pains and pleasures of social life: a social cognitive neuroscience approach." Science 323, no. 5916 (2009): 890-891. https://doi.org/10.1126/science.1170008.

Mineo, Liz, "Good Genes are Nice, but Joy is Better: Harvard Study, Almost 80 Years Old, Has Proved That Embracing Community Helps Us Live Longer, and Be Happier," The Harvard Gazette, April 11, 2017, https://news.harvard.edu/gazette/story/2017/04/over-nearly-80-years-harvard-study-has-been-showing-how-to-live-a-healthy-and-happy-life/.

"One Third of Your Life is Spent at Work." Gettysburg College. Accessed August 9, 2020. https://www.gettysburg.edu/news/stories?id=79db7b34-630c-4f49-ad32-4ab9ea48e72b.

Patel, Bindra Anjali. "'Chemo Seemed Like a Vacation': When Lawyers Hit a Breaking Point." SweaTours: Law Student Well Being. September 23, 2019, podcast audio, 26:00. https://podcasts.apple.com/us/podcast/chemo-seemed-like-vacation-when-lawyers-hit-breaking/id1469113482?i=1000450857387.

Patrick (@patJD). "EVERY COMPANY: We'd like to promote mental health in the workplace. EMPLOYEES: How about hiring more people so we feel less pressured & increase our pay." Twitter, March 20, 2019. https://me.me/i/patrick-patid-every-company-wed-like-to-promote-mental-health-9f3b6627e4e3453086dedc0cf2c847ff.

Petersen, Andrea. "Mental Resilience Can Help You Through the Coronavirus Pandemic; Here's How to Build It." The Wall Street Journal. July 13, 2020. https://www.wsj.com/articles/mental-resilience-can-help-you-through-the-coronavirus-pandemic-heres-how-to-build-it-11594688401?mod=searchresults&page=1&pos=2.

"State of the American Workplace." Gallup. 2017. https://www.gallup.com/workplace/238085/state-american-workplace-report-2017.aspx.

Well-being Concepts." Centers for Disease Control and Prevention. Accessed August 3, 2020. https://www.cdc.gov/hrqol/wellbeing.htm.

Wolf, Ryan. "Wellbeing by Generation: Where Some Thrive, Others Struggle." Gallup. November 8, 2019. https://www.gallup.com/workplace/268025/wellbeing-generation-thrive-others-struggle.aspx.

Yim, Miles. "Self-Imposed Pressure, Outside Criticism Nearly Crushed a 'League of Legends' Phenom. Now He's Back." The Washington Post. July 11, 2019. https://www.washingtonpost.com/sports/2019/07/11/self-imposed-pressure-outside-criticism-nearly-crushed-league-legends-phenom-now-hes-back/.

CHAPTER 4: CROSSROADS OF DIVERSITY, INCLUSION, AND WELLBEING

Carter, R. T., Kirkinis, K., & Johnson, V. E. (2020). "Relationships Between Trauma Symptoms and Race-Based Traumatic Stress." Traumatology, 26(1), 11–18. https://doi.org/10.1037/trm0000217.

Davis, Tchiki. "What Is Well-Being? Definition, Types, and Well-Being Skills." Psychology Today. January 2, 2019. https://www.psychologytoday.com/us/blog/click-here-happiness/201901/what-is-well-being-definition-types-and-well-being-skills

Gallo, Carmine, "The Maya Angelou Quote That Will Radically Improve Your Business," Forbes, May 31, 2014, https://www.forbes.com/sites/carminegallo/2014/05/31/the-maya-angelou-quote-that-will-radically-improve-your-business/#76ce3d06118b.

Hoffower, Hillary. "The 'Loneliest Generation' Gets Lonelier: How Millennials are Dealing with the Anxieties of Isolation and the Uncertainties of Life After Quarantine." Business Insider. May 31, 2020. https://www.businessinsider.com/millennial-mental-health-coronavirus-pandemic-quarantine-2020-5.

Kamel, Hooman. "African American Patients Have Higher Risk of Stroke Recurrence Compared with White Patients." Weill Cornell Medicine. February 24, 2020. https://news.weill.cornell.edu/news/2020/02/african-american-patients-have-higher-risk-of-stroke-recurrence-compared-with-white.

"Lupus Facts and Statistics." National Resource Center on Lupus. Last modified October 6, 2016. https://www.lupus.org/resources/lupus-facts-and-statistics.

Meads, Catherine, and David Moore. "Breast Cancer in Lesbians and Bisexual Women: Systematic Review of Incidence, Prevalence and Risk Studies." BMC Public Health 13, (December 2013): 1127. https://doi.org/10.1186/1471-2458-13-1127.

Menzies, Felicity. "How Does Employee Well-Being Link to Diversity and Inclusion?" Linkedin. September 5, 2018. https://www.linkedin.com/pulse/how-does-employee-well-being-link-diversity-inclusion-menzies-fca/.

Mickey, Ethel L., Ember Skye Kanelee, and Joya Misra. "10 Small Steps for Department Chairs to Foster Inclusion." Inside Higher Ed. June 5, 2020. https://www.insidehighered.com/advice/2020/06/05/advice-department-chairs-how-foster-inclusion-among-faculty-opinion.

Milenkovic, Milja. "42 Worrying Workplace Stress Statistics." The American Institute of Stress. September 23, 2019. https://

www.stress.org/42-worrying-workplace-stress-statistics#:~:-text=83%25%20of%20US%20workers%20suffer,to%20miss%20 work%20every%20day.

Smith, Christie, and Kenji Yoshino, "Uncovering Talent: A new model of inclusion," Deloitte, 2019, https://www2.deloitte. com/content/dam/Deloitte/us/Documents/about-deloitte/ us-about-deloitte-uncovering-talent-a-new-model-of-inclu-sion.pdf.

Smith, Ray A. "For Some Black Americans, Therapy Is Gradu-ally Losing Its Stigma." The Wall Street Journal. July 13, 2020. https://www.wsj.com/articles/for-some-black-americans-ther-apy-is-gradually-losing-its-stigma-11594657327.

Vaccaro, Adam, "Why Letting Employees Be Themselves Is So Darn Good for Business," Inc, January 6, 2014, https://www. inc.com/adam-vaccaro/why-letting-employees-express-them-selves-is-good-for-business.html.

William, David R. "Why Discrimination Is a Health Issue." Robert Wood Johnson Foundation. October 24, 2017. https://www.rwjf. org/en/blog/2017/10/discrimination-is-a-health-issue.html.

"Work-Related Stress." Better Health Channel. Accessed May 31, 2012. https://www.betterhealth.vic.gov.au/health/healthyliv-ing/work-related-stress

Zawisza, Magdalena. "The Terrifying power of stereotypes—and how to deal with them." The Conversation. August 28, 2018. https://theconversation.com/the-terrifying-power-of-stereo-types-and-how-to-deal-with-them-101904.

CHAPTER 5: WHY DOES DIVERSITY MATTER?

Allport, Gordon W., The Nature of Prejudice, 25th Anniversary ed. (New York: Perseus Books, 1979), 23-24.

Brooks, Rosa, "One Reason for Police Violence? Too Many Men with Badges," The Washington Post, June 18, 2020, https://www.washingtonpost.com/outlook/2020/06/18/women-police-officers-violence/.

Brown, Brené. Dare to Lead: Brave Work. Tough Conversations. Whole Hearts. New York: Random House, 2018, 13-36.

Brown, Jennifer. Inclusion: Diversity, The New Workplace & The Will to Change. (Hartford: Publish your Purpose Press, 2016), 242-243.

"Build a Culture Where Every Employee Can Use Their Voice," Gallup, accessed July 29, 2020, https://www.gallup.com/workplace/215939/invest-diversity-inclusion.aspx?utm_source=link_wwwv9&utm_campaign=item_236264&utm_medium=copy.

DeGrassi, Sandra W., Witney Botsford Morgan, Sarah Singletary Walker, Yingchun Wang, and Isaac Sabat. "Ethical Decision-Making: Group Diversity Holds the Key." Journal of Leadership, Accountability and Ethics 9, no. 6 (2012): 51-65.http://www.na-businesspress.com/JLAE/DeGrassiSW_Web9_6_.pdf.

Glassdoor Team, "What Job Seekers Really Think About Your Diversity and Inclusion Stats," Glassdoor, November 17, 2014, https://www.glassdoor.com/employers/blog/diversity/.

Hodge, Rae,"Twitter Makes Work from Home a Permanent Change for Some Employees," CNET, May 12, 2020, https://www.cnet.com/news/twitter-makes-work-from-home-a-permanent-change-for-some-employees/.

Holger, Dieter, "The Business Case for More Diversity," The Wall Street Journal, October 26, 2019, https://www.wsj.com/articles/the-business-case-for-more-diversity-11572091200.

"Identity," Psychology Today, accessed July 29, 2020, https://www.psychologytoday.com/us/basics/identity.

Jones, Owen, "Google's Sexist Memo has Provided the Alt-Right With a New Martyr," The Guardian, August 8, 2017, https://www.theguardian.com/commentisfree/2017/aug/08/google-sexist-memo-alt-right-martyr-james-damore.

Kurtz, Annalyn, and Tal Yellin, creators, "Millennial Generation is Bigger, More Diverse than Boomers," CNN Business, accessed July 28, 2020, https://money.cnn.com/interactive/economy/diversity-millennials-boomers/.

Mendoza-Denton, Rodolfo, "This Holiday, a Toast to Cross-Race Friendship," Psychology Today,November 23, 2010, https://www.psychologytoday.com/us/blog/are-we-born-racist/201011/holiday-toast-cross-race-friendship.

Miller, Ruthie, "5 Reasons Why Diversity Drives Innovation for Small Businesses," Sales Force, May 2, 2018, https://www.salesforce.com/blog/2018/05/diversity-drives-innovation-for-small-businesses.html#:~:text=Diversity%20Helps%20Recruitment%20and%20Hiring,is%20fierce%20in%20today's%.

Moran, Gwen, "How These Top Companies Are Getting Inclusion Right," Fast Company, January 23, 2017, https://www.fastcompany.com/3067346/how-these-top-companies-are-getting-inclusion-right.

Page-Gould, Elizabeth, and Rodolfo Mendoza-Denton. "Cross-Race Relationships: An Annotated Bibliography," Elizabeth Page-Gould, last modified February 14, 2009, http://www.page-gould.com/interracialrelationships/.

Relentless Church, "Become The Bridge | A Conversation Pastor John Gray & Steven Furtick," May 31, 2020, video, 1:07:20, https://www.youtube.com/watch?v=4_m_MK_bXz0.

Smith, Christie, and Stephanie Turner, "The Radical Transformation of Diversity and Inclusion: The Millennial Influence," Billie Jean King Leadership Initiative, 2015, http://www.bjkli.org/wp-content/uploads/2015/05/report.pdf.

CHAPTER 6: WHY DOES INCLUSION MATTER?

Carr, Evan W., Andrew Reece, Gabriella Rosen Kellerman, and Alexi Robichaux, "The Value of Belonging at Work," Harvard Business Review, December 16, 2019, https://hbr.org/2019/12/the-value-of-belonging-at-work.

Cross, Rob, Reb Rebele, and Adam Grant, "Collaborative Overload," Harvard Business Review, January 2016, https://hbr.org/2016/01/collaborative-overload.

Fishbowl Media, LLC. "Fishbowl." Fishbowlapp.com, Vers. 6.2.0 (2016). https://play.google.com/store/apps/details?id=com.fishbowlmedia.fishbowl.

Fishbowl Media, LLC. "Fishbowl." Fishbowlapp.com, Vers. 6.2.0 (2016). https://play.google.com/store/apps/details?id=com.fishbowlmedia.fishbowl.

Goleman, Daniel, Destructive Emotions: A Scientific Dialogue with the Dalai Lama (New York: Bantam Books, 2003).

Goleman, Daniel, Richard E. Boyatzis, and Annie Mckee. Primal Leadership, With a New Preface by the Authors: Unleashing the Power of Emotional Intelligence (Boston: Harvard Business Review, 2013).

Grenny, Joseph, and David Maxfield, "A Study of 1,000 Employees Found That Remote Workers Feel Shunned and Left Out," Harvard Business Review, November 2, 2017, https://hbr.org/2017/11/a-study-of-1100-employees-found-that-remote-workers-feel-shunned-and-left-out.

Hadfield, Ryan. "45 Quotes from LGBTQ+ Leaders about Diversity and Inclusion in Business." Zoominfo. October 10, 2019. https://blog.zoominfo.com/diversity-and-inclusion-quotes/

"How Managers Trump Companies," Gallup, August 12, 1999, https://news.gallup.com/businessjournal/523/how-managers-trump-companies.aspx.

Mann, Annamarie, "Why We Need Best Friends at Work," Gallup, January 15, 2018, https://www.gallup.com/workplace/236213/why-need-best-friends-work.aspx.

Meyer, Erin. The Culture Map: Breaking Through the Invisible Boundaries of Global Business. Philadelphia: Perseus Books, 2014.

Ozcelik, Hakan, and Sigal G. Barsade, "No Employee an Island: Workplace Loneliness and Job Performance," Academy of Management Journal 61, no. 6 (December 2018): 2343-66, https://doi.org/10.5465/amj.2015.1066.

Perry, Rhodes. Belonging at Work: Everyday Actions You Can Take to Cultivate an Inclusive Organization. Portland: RPC Academy Press, 2018.

Scott, Nate, "The Story of how Nike Lost Stephen Curry is Unbelievable," For the Win,March 23, 2016, https://ftw.usatoday.com/2016/03/the-story-of-how-nike-lost-stephen-curry-is-unbelievable.

Sijbrandij, Sid, "Hybrid Remote Work Offers the Worst of Both Worlds," Wired, July 12, 2020, https://www.wired.com/story/hybrid-remote-work-offers-the-worst-of-both-worlds/amp.

Smith, Christie, and Kenji Yoshino. "Uncovering Talent: Rediscovering Inclusion." Deloitte. 2019. https://www2.deloitte.com/content/dam/Deloitte/us/Documents/about-deloitte/us-about-deloitte-uncovering-talent-a-new-model-of-inclusion.pdf.

"State of the American Workplace," Gallup, 2017, https://www.gallup.com/workplace/238085/state-american-workplace-report-2017.aspx.

Wahba, Phil, "The Number of Black CEOs in the Fortune 500 Remains Very Low," Fortune, June 1, 2020, https://fortune.com/2020/06/01/black-ceos-fortune-500-2020-african-american-business-leaders/#:~:text=In%20all%20there%20have%20only,peak%20was%20six%20in%202012.

Webber, Ashleigh, "Ethnicity Pay Gap Reporting: Firms Urged Not to Wait for Legislation," Personnel Today, February 26, 2020, https://www.personneltoday.com/hr/dont-wait-for-legislation-ethnicity-pay-gap-reporting/.

"Women See Another Year of Slow Gains At Law Firms," Law 360, July 23, 2017, https://www.law360.com/articles/946586.

CHAPTER 7: WHY DOES WELLBEING MATTER?

Allin, Simon. "Workplace Wellbeing Can Boost Productivity." FT Adviser, November 23, 2017. https://www.ftadviser.com/protection/2017/11/23/workplace-wellbeing-can-boost-productivity/.

American Psychological Association, "Psychologically healthy Workplaces Have Lower Turnover, Less Stress and Higher Satisfaction," 2011, https://www.apa.org/news/press/releases/phwa/satisfaction-chart.pdf.

Connor, Tanya. "Loneliness: A New Challenge for the Remote Workplace." Remote How. June 2019. https://remote-how.com/blog/remote-workplace-loneliness-challenge.

"DeMar DeRozan on inspiring Kevin Love: 'Made me Feel Pretty Damn Good'." ESPN. March 7, 2018. https://www.espn.com/nba/story/_/id/22672925/demar-derozan-grateful-inspired-kevin-love-discuss-mental-health.

De Neve, Jan Emmanuel. "Why Wellbeing Matters and How to Improve It." Said Business School, March 6, 2020. https://www.sbs.ox.ac.uk/oxford-answers/why-wellbeing-matters-and-how-improve-it.

Hickman, Adam, "Is Working Remotely Effective? Gallup Research Says Yes," Gallup, January 24, 2020, https://www.gallup.com/workplace/283985/working-remotely-effective-gallup-research-says-yes.aspx.

Kan-Sperling, Olivia, "Sick Days: Individualized Healthcare and Corporatized Well-Being," The College Hill Independent, March 15, 2018, https://www.theindy.org/1366.

Kirsh, Adam. "Why Equality and Diversity Need to be SMB Priorities, Salesforce, February 2, 2018, Salesforce. https://www.salesforce.com/blog/2018/02/why-equality-and-diversity-need-to-be-priorities.

Litt, Joanna, "'Big Law Killed My Husband': An Open Letter From a Sidley Partner's Widow," Law.com, November 12, 2018, https://www.law.com/americanlawyer/2018/11/12/big-law-killed-my-husband-an-open-letter-from-a-sidley-partners-widow/?slreturn=20200702124008.

Mckee, Annie, "Being Happy at Work Matters," Harvard Business Review, November 14, 2014, https://hbr.org/2014/11/being-happy-at-work-matters.

"Mental Health Disorder Statistics," Johns Hopkins Medicine, accessed August 2, 2020, https://www.hopkinsmedicine.org/health/wellness-and-prevention/mental-health-disorder-statistics.

"Mental Health in the Workplace," World Health Organization, May 2019, https://www.who.int/mental_health/in_the_workplace/en/.

Miller, Stephen,"Wellness Programs as an Employee Retention Tool," SHRM, January 20, 2010, https://www.shrm.org/resourcesandtools/hr-topics/benefits/pages/wellness_employeeretention.aspx.

Murthy, Vivek H. Together: The Healing Power of Human Connection in a Sometimes Lonely World (New York: Harper Wave, 2020).

"Nearly Half of American Workers See Wellness Programs as an Important Employee Retention Tool," Business Wire, January 14, 2010, https://www.businesswire.com/news/home/20100114005799/en/American-Workers-Wellness-Programs-Important-Employee-Retention.

Pfeffer, Jeffrey. Dying for a Paycheck: How Modern Management Harms Employee Health and Company Performance—and What We Can Do About It (New York: HarperCollins, 2018), 33-36.

Pfeiffer, Eric. "Man Sets House on Fire After Using Blowtorch on Spider Webs," Yahoo! News, July 10, 2012, https://news.yahoo.com/blogs/sideshow/man-sets-house-fire-trying-kill-spiders-blowtorch-233815257.html.

Raptopoulos, Lilah, and James Fontanella-Khan, "The Trillion-Dollar Taboo: Why it's Time to Stop Ignoring Mental Health at Work," Financial Times, July 10, 2019, https://www.ft.com/content/1e8293f4-a1db-11e9-974c-ad1c6ab5efd1.

Rath, Tom, and Jim Harter, "Wellbeing: The Five Essential Elements," Gallup, accessed August 3, 2020, https://www.gallup.com/press/176624/wellbeing-five-essential-elements.aspx.

"Resources." Lawyer Brain. Accessed September 5, 2020. https://www.lawyerbrain.com/resources.

"Resources." Lawyer Brain. Accessed September 5, 2020. https://www.lawyerbrain.com/resources.

Seppälä, Emma, and Kim Cameron, "Proof That Positive Work Cultures are More Productive," Harvard Business Review, December 1, 2015, https://hbr.org/2015/12/proof-that-positive-work-cultures-are-more-productive.

Stainton, Lilo H. "NJ Launches Nation's First Stress 'Resiliency' Program for Police Officers." NJ Spotlight. August 7, 2019. https://www.njspotlight.com/2019/08/19-08-06-nj-launches-nations-first-stress-resiliency-program-for-police-officers/.

Tappe, Anneken. "The Coronavirus Recession is Hitting Women the Hardest." CNN Business. May 11, 2020. https://www.cnn.

com/2020/05/11/economy/women-disadvantaged-econo-my-coronavirus/index.html.

"Well-being Concepts," Centers for Disease Control and Prevention, accessed August 3, 2020, https://www.cdc.gov/hrqol/wellbeing. html.

CHAPTER 8: HOW TO IMPROVE DIVERSITY

Bembry, Jerry, "Mavericks' Cynthia Marshall: 'I Want to Do it For the Sisterhood,'" The Undefeated, February 27, 2018, https:// theundefeated.com/features/mavericks-interim-ceo-marshall-i-want-to-do-it-for-the-sisterhood/.

"By 2050 There Will be No Clear Racial or Ethnic Majority in our Nation." Center for American Progress. April 2012. https://www.americanprogress.org/wp-content/uploads/ issues/2012/04/pdf/progress_2050_one_pager.pdf.

Draznin, Haley. "The Dallas Mavericks Were Plagued by a Toxic Culture. She is Turning it Around." CNN Business. November 19,2019. https://www.cnn.com/2019/09/30/success/dallas-mavericks-ceo-cynthia-marshall-boss-files/index.html.

Dutta, Darshana. "25 Powerful Diversity and Inclusion Quotes for a Stronger Company Culture." Vantage Circle. Last modified June 18, 2020. https://blog.vantagecircle.com/diversity-and-in-clusion-quotes/.

Ferguson, Deborah, "Mavs CEO Celebrates Completion of 100-Day Plan to Change Workplace Culture," NBC Dallas-Fort Worth,

August 17, 2018, https://www.nbcdfw.com/news/local/mavs-ceo-celebrates-completion-of-100-day-plan/77453/.

Goodman, Matt. "Meet Cynt Marshall, the Woman Who Mark Cuban Hopes Can Fix the Mavericks' Culture." D Magazine. February 26, 2018. https://www.dmagazine.com/frontburner/2018/02/meet-cynt-marshall-the-woman-who-mark-cuban-hopes-can-fix-the-mavericks-culture.

Harlow, Poppy, host, "Cynthia Marshall: Rebuilding the Dallas Mavericks," September 30, 2019, in Boss Files, podcast audio, 53:00, https://podcasts.apple.com/us/podcast/cynthia-marshall-rebuilding-the-dallas-mavericks/id1201282406?i=1000451753068.

"How We Make Textio," Textio, accessed August 8, 2020, https://textio.com/principles/.

Knobler, Leah, "Diversity and Inclusion at Help Scout: 2018 Update," Help Scout, August 16, 2018, https://www.helpscout.com/blog/diversity-inclusion-2018/.

Marshall, Cynt. Cynt Marshall to Anne. Letter. From Rack CDN. Accessed September 5, 2020. https://f1f64ea4c4b583b18306-3f73a7ab3eff14b4728a55d6928da99b.ssl.cf5.rackcdn.com/Letter-from-Cynt-Marshall.PDF.

Marshall, Cynt. Cynt Marshall to Anne. Letter. From Rack CDN. Accessed September 5, 2020. https://f1f64ea4c4b583b18306-3f73a7ab3eff14b4728a55d6928da99b.ssl.cf5.rackcdn.com/Letter-from-Cynt-Marshall.PDF.

Mohr, Tara Sophia. "Why Women Don't Apply for Jobs Unless They're 100% Qualified." Harvard Business Review. August 25, 2014. https://hbr.org/2014/08/why-women-dont-apply-for-jobs-unless-theyre-100-qualified.

"Monster's 2020 State of the Candidate Survey Highlights." Monster. Accessed August 7, 2020. https://hiring.monster.com/employer-resources/uncategorized/monsters-2020-state-of-the-candidate-infographic/.

O'Mara, Kelly Dunleavy. "Always a Maverick: Cynthia Marshall Made Her Mark Before Dallas." UC Berkeley. September 28, 2018. https://alumni.berkeley.edu/california-magazine/just-in/2018-09-28/always-maverick-cynthia-marshall-made-her-mark-dallas.

Rader, Doyle. "Dallas Mavericks Pledge to Pay Arena Staff for Six Postponed Home Games." Forbes. March 13, 2020. https://www.forbes.com/sites/doylerader/2020/03/13/dallas-mavericks-american-airlines-center-staff-will-receive-pay-six-home-games/#406c0c0177b5.

"Reach for the Stars: Realizing the Potential of America's Hidden Talent Pool." Opportunity at Work. March 2020. https://opportunityatwork.org/wp-content/uploads/2020/03/Opportunity-At-Work-Report-Reach-for-the-STARs-FINAL.pdf.

Renken, Elena. "How Stories Connect And Persuade Us: Unleashing The Brain Power of Narrative." NPR. April 11, 2020. https://www.npr.org/sections/health-shots/2020/04/11/815573198/how-stories-connect-and-persuade-us-unleashing-the-brain-power-of-narrative.

Scipioni, Jade, "Dallas Mavericks CEO to leaders: 'This is Our Moment. Don't Miss It,'" CNBC, last modified June 18, 2020, https://www.cnbc.com/2020/06/03/mavericks-ceo-marshall-to-leaders-this-is-our-moment-dont-miss-it.html.

Scipioni, Jade, "Dallas Mavericks CEO to leaders: 'This is Our Moment. Don't Miss It,'" CNBC, last modified June 18, 2020, https://www.cnbc.com/2020/06/03/mavericks-ceo-marshall-to-leaders-this-is-our-moment-dont-miss-it.html.

Scipioni, Jade. "From the First Black Cheerleader at Berkeley Making History as Mavericks CEO: How Cynt Marshall Did It." CNBC. February 21, 2020. https://www.cnbc.com/2020/02/21/mavericks-cynt-marshall-first-black-woman-ceo-in-the-nba-on-success.html.

Stephens, Greg J., Lauren J. Silbert, and Uri Hasson. "Speaker-Listener Neural Coupling Underlies Successful Communication." Proceedings of the National Academy of Sciences of the United States of America 107, 32 (August 2010): 14425-30. https://doi.org/10.1073/pnas.1008662107.

"The Report of the Independent Investigation of Dallas Basketball Limited." Courthouse News. September 19, 2018. https://www.courthousenews.com/wp-content/uploads/2018/09/DallasMavericks.pdf.

Townsend, Brad, "One Year Later: How the Mavs' Culture Transformed from 'Corrosive' to Inclusive," The Dallas Morning News, September 18, 2019, https://www.dallasnews.com/sports/mavericks/2019/09/18/one-year-later-how-the-mavs-culture-transformed-from-corrosive-to-inclusive/.

Wertheim, Jon, and Jessica Luther, "Exclusive: Inside the Corrosive Workplace Culture of the Dallas Mavericks," Sports Illustrated, February 20, 2018, https://www.si.com/nba/2018/02/21/dallas-mavericks-sexual-misconduct-investigation-mark-cuban-response.

Wertheim, Jon, and Jessica Luther, "Exclusive: Inside the Corrosive Workplace Culture of the Dallas Mavericks," Sports Illustrated, February 20, 2018, https://www.si.com/nba/2018/02/21/dallas-mavericks-sexual-misconduct-investigation-mark-cuban-response.

Yip, Sam. "'Everything Went to Hell': Stadium Workers on the US Sports Shutdown." The Guardian. March 24, 2020. https://www.theguardian.com/sport/2020/mar/24/arena-stadium-workers-coronavirus-covid-19-outbreak-sports-shutdown.

CHAPTER 9 : HOW TO IMPROVE INCLUSION

Bilkhu, Raj Kaur. "Shaadi.com: Dating Site Removes Skin Tone Filter After Backlash." BBC News. June 23, 2020. https://www.bbc.com/news/newsbeat-53146969.

Brown, Brené, The Gifts of Imperfection: Let Go of Who You Think You're Supposed to Be and Embrace Who You Are (Center City: Hazelden Publishing, 2010),26.

Brown, Joel. The Diversity Collegium. Accessed September 6, 2020. http://diversitycollegium.org/profiles/joel_brown.php.

Carlson, Gretchen. It's time to Lift Our Voices", accessed August 8, 2020, https://www.gretchencarlson.com/voices2.

Coll, Ally, and Shea Holman, "Steps to Maintain Workplace Equality During The Pandemic," Law360, April 27, 2020, https://www.law360.com/articles/1266964/steps-to-maintain-workplace-equality-during-the-pandemic.

Cuban, Brian, "Creating Compassionate Community in the Legal Profession," Briancuban.com, February 21, 2020, https://briancuban.com/blog/creating-compassionate-community-in-the-legal-profession/.

"Dashanne Stokes Quotes," Dashannestokes.com, accessed August 8, 2020, http://www.dashannestokes.com/quotes.html.

E. W., "What's Holding Women Back?," The Economist, January 23, 2015, https://www.economist.com/democracy-in-america/2015/01/23/whats-holding-women-back.

Ferrazzi, Keith, "Getting Virtual Teams Right," Harvard Business Review, December 2014, https://hbr.org/2014/12/getting-virtual-teams-right.

Gates, Bill, and Gates, Melinda, "2014 Commencement Address," June 15, 2014, Stanford University, Stanford, CA, speech transcript, https://news.stanford.edu/news/2014/june/gates-commencement-remarks-061514.html.

Gladwell, Malcolm, Talking to Strangers: What We Should Know about the People we Don't Know (New York: Hachette, 2019), 352.

Heckman, August W., III, Thomas A. Linthorst, and Richard G. Rosenblatt, "New Jersey Bans Some Nondisclosure and

Waiver Provisions," Morgan Lewis, March 25, 2019, https://www.morganlewis.com/pubs/new-jersey-bans-some-nondisclosure-and-waiver-provisions.

Hoffman, Reid, Ben Casnocha, and Chris Yeh. The Alliance: Managing Talent in the Networked Age. Boston: Harvard Business Review Press, 2014.

"Home." The Purple Campaign. Accessed September 6, 2020. https://www.purplecampaign.org/.

Lapchick, Richard. "How sports is helping Orlando heal." ESPN. June 20, 2016. https://www.espn.com/espn/story/_/id/16370274/how-sports-heal-unite-change-society-forever.

Moyler, Hunter, "Gretchen Carlson Calls on Mike Bloomberg To Free Women From the NDAs They Signed While Working For Him," Newsweek, February 3, 2020, https://www.newsweek.com/gretchen-carlson-calls-mike-bloomberg-free-women-ndas-they-signed-while-working-him-1485475.

Murthy, Vivek H. Together: The Healing Power of Human Connection in a Sometimes Lonely World (New York: Harper Wave, 2020), 121-23.

"Non-Disclosure Agreements (NDAs)," Workplace Fairness, accessed August 8, 2020, https://www.workplacefairness.org/nondisclosure-agreements.

Ross, Howard. "Don't Let Divisions Lead to Workplace Dysfunction." SHRM. May 9, 2018. https://www.shrm.org/hr-today/

news/hr-magazine/book-blog/pages/dont-let-divisions-lead-to-workforce-dysfunction.aspx.

Shaw, Elyse, Ariane Hegewisch, and Cynthia Hess. "Sexual Harassment and Assault at Work: Understanding the Costs." Institute for Womens Policy Research. October 2018. https://iwpr.org/wp-content/uploads/2020/09/IWPR-sexual-harassment-brief_FINAL.pdf.

Silver-Greenberg, Jessica, and Natalie Kitroeff, "How Bloomberg Buys the Silence of Unhappy Employees," New York Times, last modified March 4, 2020, https://www.nytimes.com/2020/03/02/business/michael-bloomberg-nda.html.

Swirling, Robyn, "Sexual Harassment Still Happens When You Work from Home During a Pandemic," Medium, March 17, 2020, https://medium.com/swlh/sexual-harassment-still-happens-when-you-work-from-home-during-a-pandemic-3bba3e230399.

CHAPTER 10: HOW TO INCREASE INCLUSIVE RECRUITING

"Asilomar AI Principles." Future of Life Institute. Accessed August 9, 2020. https://futureoflife.org/ai-principles/?submitted=1#confirmation.

"Barriers and Bias: The Status of Women in Leadership," American Association of University of Women, accessed April 5, 2020, https://www.aauw.org/app/uploads/2020/03/Barriers_and_Bias_summary.pdf.

BasuMallick, Chiradeep, "4 Workplace Diversity Trends for 2019," HR Technologist, December 18, 2018, https://www.hrtechnologist.com/articles/employee-engagement/4-workplace-diversity-trends-for-2019/.

Bertrand, Marianne, and Sendhil Mullainathan, "Are Emily and Greg More Employable than Lakisha and Jamal? A Field Experiment on Labor Market Discrimination,"American Economic Review 94, no. 4 (September 2004): 991-1013, https://doi.org/10.1257/0002828042002561.

Cappelli, Peter, "Your Approach to Hiring Is All Wrong," Harvard Business Review, May 2019, https://hbr.org/2019/05/recruiting#data-science-cant-fix-hiring-yet.

Francis, David R. "Employers' Replies to Racial Names." The National Bureau of Economic Research. Accessed September 6, 2020. https://www.nber.org/digest/sep03/w9873.html.

Gerson Lehrman Group, Inc., "Neuroscientist Vivienne Ming Discusses 'The Tax on Being Different' And How Big Data Helps Maximize Human Potential," PR Newswire, June 27, 2017, https://www.prnewswire.com/news-releases/neuroscientist-vivienne-ming-discusses-the-tax-on-being-different-and-how-big-data-helps-maximize-human-potential-300479760.html.

"How We Make Textio," Textio, accessed August 8, 2020, https://textio.com/principles/.

Jones-Sawyer, Reggie, and Julian Canete, "La Opinión: How to End Biased Hiring in California," Fair Hiring California, September 6, 2019, https://fairhiringca.com/how-to-end-biased-hiring-in-california/.

Kane, Margaret, "Say What? 'Young People are just smarter,'" CNET, March 28, 2007, https://www.cnet.com/news/say-what-young-people-are-just-smarter/.

"Language Matters: How Words Impact Men and Women in the Workplace," Linkedin Business, accessed August 9, 2020, https://business.linkedin.com/content/me/business/en-us/talent-solutions/recruiting-tips/gender-insights-language-matters?u=0.

Ming, Vivienne, "From Cognitive Modeling to Labor Markets" (EdLab Seminar, Vialogues, April 1, 2015), https://www.vialogues.com/vialogues/play/21460/.

Ming, Vivienne, "The Hidden Tax on Being Different," HR Magazine, November 23, 2016, https://www.hrmagazine.co.uk/article-details/the-hidden-tax-on-being-different.

Ming, Vivienne. "There is a Tax on Being Different," Financial Times, July 3, 2016. https://www.ft.com/content/1929cd86-3eb6-11e6-8716-a4a71e8140b0.

Moss-Racusin, Corinne A., John F. Dovidio, Victoria L. Brescoll, Mark J. Graham, and Jo Handelsman. "Science faculty's subtle gender biases favor male students." Proceedings of the National Academy of Sciences of the United States of America 109, no. 41(October 2012): 16474-79. https://doi.org/10.1073/pnas.1211286109.

Neumark, David, Ian Burn, and Patrick Button, "Age Discrimination and Hiring Older Workers," Federal Reserve Bank of San Francisco, February 27, 2017, https://www.frbsf.org/economic-research/files/el2017-06.pdf.

O'Brien, Sara Ashely, "Women coders do better than men in gender-blind study," CNN Money, February 12, 2016, https://money.cnn.com/2016/02/12/technology/women-coders-study-github/index.html.

Palmer, Kimberly, "10 Things You Should Know About Age Discrimination," AARP, February 20, 2017, https://www.aarp.org/work/on-the-job/info-2017/age-discrimination-facts.html.

Patel, Bindra Anjali. "Artificial Intelligence: Unleashing Human Potential." SweaTours: Law Student Well Being. December 2, 2019. Podcast audio, 35:39. https://podcasts.apple.com/us/podcast/artificial-intelligence-unleashing-human-potential/id1469113482?i=1000458458649.

Phillips, Katherine W., "How Diversity Makes Us Smarter," Scientific American, October 1, 2014, https://www.scientificamerican.com/article/how-diversity-makes-us-smarter/.

Polli, Frida, "Using AI to Eliminate Bias from Hiring," Harvard Business Review, October 29, 2019, https://hbr.org/2019/10/using-ai-to-eliminate-bias-from-hiring.

Rivera, Lauren,"Firms Are Wasting Millions Recruiting on Only a Few Campuses," Harvard Business Review, October 23, 2015, https://hbr.org/2015/10/firms-are-wasting-millions-recruiting-on-only-a-few-campuses.

"Robert Frost Quotes." Brainy Quote. Accessed September 6, 2020. https://www.brainyquote.com/authors/robert-frost-quotes.

Sabel, Jon-Mark, "How AI is Transforming Pre-Hire Assessments [Webinar Recap]," HireVue, August 24, 2017, https://www.hirevue.com/blog/how-ai-is-transforming-pre-hire-assessments-webinar-recap.

Terrell, Kenneth, "Age Bias Complaints Rise Among Women and Minorities," AARP, June 28, 2018, https://www.aarp.org/work/working-at-50-plus/info-2018/age-discrimination-increases-women-minorities.html.

Terrell, Kenneth, "Age Bias That's Barred by Law Appears in Thousands of Job Listings," AARP, October 30, 2019, https://www.aarp.org/work/working-at-50-plus/info-2019/age-bias-job-listings.html.

"Women in Leadership: Tackling Corporate Culture from the Top." Rockefeller Foundation. Accessed September 6, 2020. https://www.rockefellerfoundation.org/wp-content/uploads/Women-in-Leadership-Tackling-Corporate-Culture-from-the-Top.pdf.

CHAPTER 11: HOW TO IMPROVE WELLBEING

Brower, Holly Henderson, Scott Wayne Lester, and M. Audrey Korsgaard, "Want Your Employees to Trust You? Show You Trust Them," Harvard Business Review, July 5, 2017, https://hbr.org/2017/07/want-your-employees-to-trust-you-show-you-trust-them.

Brown, Brené, The Gifts of Imperfection: Let Go of Who You Think You're Supposed to Be and Embrace Who You Are (Center City: Hazelden Publishing, 2010),26.

Butkovich, Sasha, "Ways to improve Your Mental Health on Your Lunch Break," Justworks, April 30, 2020, https://justworks.com/blog/improve-mental-health-work-midday-break-ideas.

Connley, Courtney. "Why the CEO of Basecamp Only Allows Employees to Work 32 Hours a Week." CNBC. Last modified August 4, 2017. https://www.cnbc.com/2017/08/03/the-ceo-of-basecamp-only-allows-employees-to-put-in-a-32-hour-work-week.html.

"Depression Symptom Checklist," Trintellix, accessed August 9, 2020, https://us.trintellix.com/depression-symptom-check-list?utm_term=sign%20of%20depression&utm_content=349091606828&utm_adid=70404779757&utm_source=google&utm_medium.

Drechsler, Paul. Obsidian Systems (@obsidianza). "'Good Health IS Good Business.' Chairman/CEO, Wates Group Limited A Reminder on #WorldHealthDay that a physically healthy workforce contributes to Healthy and Thriving business." Twitter, April 7, 2020. https://twitter.com/obsidianza/status/1247480873651503104.

Gartner, Inc. "Gartner Survey Reveals 82% of Company Leaders Plan to Allow Employees to Work Remotely Some of the Time." Gartner. July 14, 2020. https://www.gartner.com/en/newsroom/press-releases/2020-07-14-gartner-survey-reveals-

82-percent-of-company-leaders-plan-to-allow-employees-to-work-remotely-some-of-the-time.

MacLellan, Lila, "Google is Running an Employee Mental Health Project Without any Metrics," Quartz at Work, June 25, 2019, https://qz.com/work/1650113/googles-blue-dot-mental-health-project-promotes-compassionate-listening/.

MacLellan, Lila, "Millennials Experience Work-Disrupting Anxiety at Twice the US average Rate," Quartz at Work, December 5, 2018, https://qz.com/work/1483697/millennials-experience-work-disrupting-anxiety-at-twice-the-us-average-rate/.

Moskowitz, Dan. "The 5 Richest People in the World." Investopedia. Last modified March 30, 2020. https://www.investopedia.com/articles/investing/012715/5-richest-people-world.asp.

Patel, Bindra Anjali, "Lisa Smith: From Breaking Down to Breaking Through," December 9, 2019, in SweaTours: Law Student Well Being, podcast audio, 26:00, https://podcasts.apple.com/us/podcast/lisa-smith-from-breaking-down-to-breaking-through/id1469113482?i=1000459135589.

Pentland, Alex, "The New Science of Building Great Teams," Harvard Business Review, April 2012, https://hbr.org/2012/04/the-new-science-of-building-great-teams.

"Sleep Deprivation: An Oft-Ignored Occupational Hazard in Health Care." Healio News, May 10, 2017. https://www.healio.com/news/cardiac-vascular-intervention/20170510/sleep-deprivation-an-oftignored-occupational-hazard-in-health-care.

Smith, Lisa, Girl Walks Out of a Bar: A Memoir (New York: Select-Books, 2016), 150.

"Trends and Insights on the Small Business Economy," Emergent Research, accessed August 9, 2020, http://www.emergentresearch.com/.

Waber, Ben, Jennifer Magnolfi, and Greg Lindsay, "Workplaces That Move People," Harvard Business Review, October 2014, https://hbr.org/2014/10/workspaces-that-move-people.

Whalen, Robyn, "The Role of Financial Health in Employee Wellbeing," Total Wellness, August 7, 2017, https://info.total-wellnesshealth.com/blog/the-role-of-financial-health-in-employee-wellbeing.

CONCLUSION: WHERE DO WE GO FROM HERE?

Brewer, Josh, "Inclusion is a Choice," Abstract, January 17, 2019, https://www.abstract.com/blog/inclusion-is-a-choice.

Hutrya, Hanna. "123 of the Most Inspiring Martia Luther King Jr. Quotes," Accessed June 1, 2020. https://www.keepinspiring.me/martin-luther-king-jr-quotes/.

Mackey, John, and Rajendra Sisodia, Conscious Capitalism: Liberating the Heroic Spirit of Business (Boston: Harvard Business Review Press, 2013), 209.